S268 Physical Resources and Environment
Science: a second level course

4
BLOCK

ENERGY 2

NUCLEAR AND ALTERNATIVES

Prepared for the Course Team by Geoff Brown and John Wright

S268 Physical Resources and Environment

Course Team

Dave Williams (Course Chair)
Andrew Bell
Geoff Brown
Steve Drury
Chris Hawkesworth
Ian Nuttall (Editor)
Janice Robertson (Editor)
Peter Sheldon
Sandy Smith
Peter Webb
Chris Wilson
John Wright
Annemarie Hedges (Course Manager)
Charlie Bendall (Course Coordinator)

Production

Jane Sheppard (Graphic Designer)
Steve Best (Graphic Artist)
David Jackson (Series Producer, BBC)
Nicholas Watson (BBC Producer)
John Greenwood (Liaison Librarian)
Eira Parker (Course Secretary)
Marilyn Leggett (Secretary)
Lynn Tilbury (Secretary)

Course assessor

Professor Peter W. Scott, Camborne School of Mines.

Dedication

Professor Geoff Brown was a member of the Course Team when he was killed on the Galeras Volcano, Colombia, in January 1993. The Course Team dedicates S268 to his memory.

Acknowledgements

The Course Team gratefully acknowledges the contributions of members of the S238 course team (S238 *The Earth's Physical Resources*, 1984).

The Course Team also wishes to thank Sheila Dellow for careful reading of early drafts of the course material.

The Open University, Walton Hall, Milton Keynes MK7 6AA.

First published 1995.

Edited, designed and typeset by The Open University.

Printed in the United Kingdom by Henry Ling Limited, The Dorset Press, Dorchester.

ISBN 0 7492 5149 2

This text forms part of an Open University second level course. If you would like a copy of Studying with the Open University, please write to the Central Enquiry Service, PO Box 200, The Open University, Walton Hall, Milton Keynes, MK7 6YZ. If you have not already enrolled on the course and would like to buy this or other Open University material, please write to Open University Educational Enterprises Ltd, 12 Cofferidge Close, Stony Stratford, Milton Keynes, MK11 1BY, United Kingdom.

Edition 1.1

S268block4part2i1.1

CONTENTS

1 INTRODUCTION

As we learned in the first part of Block 4 on fossil fuels, over 85% of the energy requirements of our modern civilization comes from coal, oil and gas. Use of these fossil fuels began in a small way many centuries ago, supplementing the historically traditional exploitation of animals (for draught and transport), wood (for cooking and heating), wind (sailing vessels, windmills) and water (waterwheels, tidal mills). The Industrial Revolution revolutionized patterns of energy use. The exponential increase in the contribution of fossil fuels to 'feed the fires of industry' stems from that time.

Fossil fuels are non-renewable resources; they took millions of years to form, and they are being used at rates that will deplete reserves in a matter of a few generations. Moreover, as they are carbon-based fuels, their combustion increases the atmospheric concentration of the greenhouse gas CO_2. There is widespread concern that continued use of fossil fuels at present rates will lead to global warming, with climatic consequences that are difficult to foresee.

So what is the alternative? Are there other sources of energy that can supplement and eventually replace the fossil fuels, and are they sufficient to sustain our needs?

This Block addresses those questions. We begin by reviewing the short but chequered history of nuclear power, which has been with us for barely half a century, for it grew out of the atomic weapons technology of the Second World War. Although its star is no longer in the ascendant as we approach the end of the second millennium, it receives more than superficial treatment in this Block, for two important reasons: first, it still provides a sizeable proportion of the energy needs of several countries; and second, there are still plenty of industrialists, politicians and others who believe it will make an essential contribution to future energy supplies. If energy requirements continue at present levels, nuclear power is one of the very few options available to sustain those requirements as fossil fuels become depleted. The reason is that prodigious amounts of energy are liberated per unit mass of nuclear fuel — orders of magnitude more than with any of the fossil fuels. In addition, although undesirable radioactive waste products may be associated with this technology, nuclear power stations emit neither CO_2 nor the gases that contribute to acid rain (sulphur and nitrogen oxides).

However, should society be forced to do without fossil fuels (which must happen sooner or later, one way or another) and decide also to eschew the nuclear option, the only alternative presently available may be a return to reliance on the 'traditional' pre-industrial forms of energy, albeit with the improvements that industrial technology can bring to their deployment. These largely renewable and (in the main) environmentally benign alternatives are reviewed in the middle Sections of the Block: geothermal and solar energy, biomass burning, wind (including wave) power, and water (including tidal) power. They already contribute a significant proportion of regional or even national energy needs in several countries. The problem is that, as we saw in Block 4 *Energy 1 – Fossil Fuels*, they are relatively 'dilute' sources of energy compared with fossil (not to mention nuclear) fuels and their energy cannot easily be stored or transported. Reliance on them for the bulk of our energy needs would therefore necessitate great reductions in demand and/or great increases in energy efficiency and conservation.

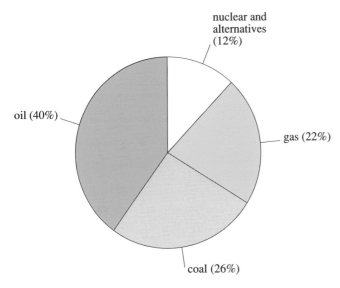

Figure 1 Approximate percentage contributions of different energy resources to the global power requirements (mid-1990s) of about 10^{13} W ($\approx 3.5 \times 10^{20}$ J y^{-1}).

If we look further ahead, the most promising — and as yet largely untapped — source of energy available to us is hydrogen, limitless in quantity and virtually 'pure' in environmental terms. This alternative is briefly explored in the last Section of the Block, along with a discussion of energy needs, past, present and future, including an assessment of the extent to which humanity is equipping itself to cope with the implications of sustainable development.

A note on terms and units

As defined in Block 4 *Energy 1*, *energy* is the capacity to do work, and the unit is the joule (J); and *power* is the rate at which work is done or at which energy is converted from one form to another, and the unit is the watt (W), 1 W = 1 J s^{-1}. In this Block we use these units most of the time, but it is sometimes convenient to use the hybrid of energy delivered in unit time, such as a day or year (J day^{-1}, J y^{-1}). We sometimes also use kWh (kilowatt hour) as a unit of energy, which should be familiar from domestic fuel bills. 1 kWh = 3.6×10^6 J.

In everyday conversation, the terms 'energy' and 'power' are often used interchangeably and people sometimes say energy when they mean power and *vice versa*. There may be the occasional lapse from rigorous use of the terms in this Block, but the meaning should be clear from the context.

Some useful numbers

Energy in radioactive decay of uranium-238 = 3×10^3 J kg^{-1} y^{-1}

Energy from combustion of coal = 2.8×10^7 J kg^{-1}

Fission energy of uranium-235 = 8.2×10^{13} J kg^{-1}

World energy demand (1993) = $\sim 3.5 \times 10^{20}$ J y^{-1} ($\sim 3.9 \times 10^{20}$ J y^{-1} if subsistence biomass burning included)

Global heat flow average = 60 mW m^{-2}

1 watt = 1 joule per second (1 W = 1 J s^{-1})

1 kilowatt hour (1 kWh) = 3.6×10^6 J

1 kilowatt (kW) = 10^3 W

1 megawatt (MW) = 10^6 W

1 gigawatt (GW) = 10^9 W = 31.5×10^{15} J y^{-1}

2 NUCLEAR ENERGY

As we will see in later Sections, the breakdown of heavy unstable uranium isotopes provides vastly more energy per unit mass of fuel than any other energy source (except nuclear fusion; see Section 5.2.1), and therein lies its attraction. In Section 1.3.1 of Block 4 *Energy 1*, we read:

> When Einstein formulated his famous equation $E = mc^2$, he showed that mass and energy are proportional to one another (the constant linking the two is the square of the speed of light). Scientists now realize that the conversion of matter (with mass, m) into energy (E, in joules) is one of the most exciting future energy-producing possibilities.

In fact, scientists have realized this since the early years of the twentieth century, and the potential energy-producing processes became real when the first ever atomic pile 'went critical' in December 1942. The nuclear power programme expanded rapidly in the 1960s, a period when the costs of building nuclear power stations and of purchasing the uranium fuel were stated to be less than for fossil fuel plants. The nuclear industry received a boost in the early 1970s, when fossil fuel prices rose abruptly during the 'oil crisis' (oil producers in the Middle East quadrupled the price of their crude oil almost overnight).

During the 1980s, however, the costs of building nuclear power stations rose inexorably as requirements for improved safety standards became ever more stringent, especially following the accident at Three Mile Island in Pennsylvania (1979) and the much larger one at Chernobyl (1986) in the Ukraine. In addition, the cost of decommissioning nuclear reactors and of finding repositories for radioactive waste products was initially not taken into account in cost–benefit analyses, but has loomed progressively larger as older nuclear power stations approach the end of their useful lives and as the volume of waste grows year by year. The rate of expansion of the nuclear industry had slowed almost to a standstill by the early 1990s, and as demand for uranium fuel fell, so did its price — in other words, the fuel got cheaper as the power stations became more expensive.

The declining fortunes of the nuclear industry can be attributed in part to public concerns about accidents at power stations, about the safe disposal of radioactive wastes, and about the proliferation of weapons stemming from the wider availability of nuclear fuels (an issue which survived the end of the Cold War), and in part to escalating costs caused by unexpected technical problems, not least those related to requirements for operational safety.

These concerns have tended to obscure the big environmental advantage that nuclear power has over fossil fuels: it produces no acid rain or greenhouse gases (except where fossil fuel energy is used for extraction and processing of nuclear fuel). But as you will see, the 'mix' of energy sources that should be used for future power generation will be determined more by social, political and economic factors — perhaps even by environmental considerations — than by the nature and geological origin and availability of the energy sources themselves.

In the mid-1990s over 400 electricity generating nuclear reactors were in operation around the world, producing over 300 GW (Table 1). This amounts to about 16% of global electricity generating capacity, and about 3% of total global energy requirements. Many of the UK's reactors are of an early design and only a few of the younger nuclear power stations match the 1 GW capacity of most fossil fuel stations. Nevertheless, well over 20% of UK electricity generating capacity is nuclear; we shall consider the advantages and limitations of this situation shortly.

Table 1 Nuclear reactors and generating capacity in 1990

	Reactors in operation	Electricity generated/MW	Percentage of total electricity produced
North and Central America			
Canada	18	12 185	15.6
Mexico	1	654	5 (estimated)
USA	110	98 331	19.1
South America			
Argentina	2	935	11.4
Brazil	1	626	0.7
Europe			
Belgium	7	5 500	60.8
Bulgaria	5	2 585	32.9
Czechoslovakia	8	3 264	27.6
Finland	4	2 310	35.4
France	55	52 588	74.6
Germany	30	24 817	29.0
Hungary	4	1 645	49.8
Italy	2	1 120	5 (estimated)
Netherlands	2	508	5.4
Spain	10	7 544	38.4
Sweden	12	9 817	45.1
Switzerland	5	2 952	41.6
UK	39	11 242	21.7
Yugoslavia	1	632	5.9
Asia			
India	7	1 374	1.6
Japan	39	29 300	27.8
Pakistan	1	125	0.2
South Korea	9	7 220	50.2
Taiwan	6	4 924	35.2
Soviet Republics	46	34 230	12.3
Africa			
South Africa	2	1 842	7.4
totals	426	318 270	(world) ~16

Source: International Atomic Energy Agency, Vienna.

2.1 Nuclear reactions, reactors and power generation

The nuclear reactions that produce the energy from uranium fuel are complex (Section 2.1.1) but the actual generation of electricity is no different in principle from what goes on in fossil fuel power stations (Figure 2). In both cases the fuel (whether fossil or nuclear) is used to heat water in a steam boiler. The steam is piped at high pressure into the generating plant to drive turbines which generate the electricity. The steam is then condensed, often with the aid of cooling towers (Figure 2) and the condensed water is returned to the boiler for reheating. This is a closed circuit, and the water never comes in contact with the fuel (unless there is a leak, which requires immediate shut-down until repairs can be effected).

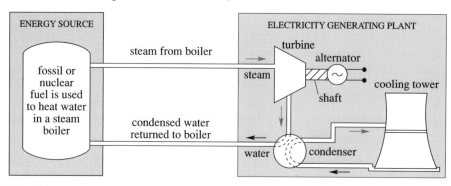

Figure 2 The basic pattern of an electricity generating plant, using either fossil or nuclear fuel.

Efficiency of power stations

As outlined in the first chapter of Block 4 *Energy 1*, the efficiency with which power stations convert their source of heat — be it fossil or nuclear fuel or any other kind of energy source — into electricity, is defined as

$$\text{efficiency} = \frac{\text{electrical power out}}{\text{heat produced}} \times 100\%$$

In general, power station efficiency is between 30% and 40%. The other 60–70% of the energy is transferred as heat to the cooling water of the condenser when the steam is liquefied, and is then carried away.

The principal way in which the efficiency of a power station can be maximized is to have the temperature of the steam going into the turbines high as possible. The steam from fossil-fuelled power stations is at about 600 °C, which is as high as is practicable;

at this temperature the efficiency of the power station is about 40%. If the steam temperature is 350 °C, the efficiency drops to about 30%.

Turbines cannot extract more energy from the steam because of the thermodynamics of such systems. The efficiency of conversion depends upon the ratio of the temperature of the steam entering the turbine to that of the steam leaving it, measured from absolute zero (0 on the Kelvin temperature scale, or −273 °C): the greater this ratio, the higher the efficiency. In any power station, the temperature of the steam leaving the turbines is considerably greater than that of the surroundings (hence the need for condensers), i.e. considerably more than 300 °C above absolute zero.

In *combined heat and power stations*, some of the waste heat is used to heat buildings. This increases the total percentage of heat used usefully, but decreases the amount of electricity produced.

2.1.1 Nuclear fission

In the opening sentence of Section 2, we mentioned 'heavy unstable uranium isotopes'. What do we mean by these terms? Going back to fundamentals, we read in Block 1 that every atom of a chemical element has a *nucleus* consisting of positively charged *protons* and electrically neutral *neutrons*. Protons and neutrons have virtually identical mass and the total number of protons and neutrons defines the **mass number** of a particular atom. The number of protons in the nucleus is the **atomic number** and this quantity is always the same for any particular chemical element. However, elements may have different **isotopes** in which the number of neutrons varies, while the number of protons stays the same. From our point of view, uranium has two isotopes of interest:

uranium-235, which has 92 protons and 143 neutrons, written $^{235}_{92}$U

uranium-238, which also has 92 protons but 146 neutrons, written $^{238}_{92}$U

i.e. both isotopes have the same atomic number (92) but different mass numbers (235 and 238).

These isotopes have such large nuclei that they are inherently unstable. They spontaneously break down, or decay, by two processes:

1 **radioactive decay**, a process that emits **alpha particles**, which are equivalent to the nuclei of helium atoms, with two protons and two neutrons, $^{4}_{2}$He;

2 **fission**, a much less frequent process, in which the whole nucleus breaks apart, releasing energy.

● But how does nuclear fission release energy?

○ The products of nuclear fission (*daughter* products) are nuclei of other elements whose combined mass totals slightly less than the mass of the parent uranium nucleus. The 'missing' mass is converted to energy according to the relationship $E = mc^2$, where m is the 'missing' mass, and c is the speed of light. Because the speed of light is so enormous (3×10^8 m s^{-1}), when the number is squared, even a small mass converts to a huge amount of energy, as we saw in Block 4 *Energy 1*.

Of the naturally occurring radioactive elements, only uranium and thorium undergo spontaneous fission and release energy on this potentially vast scale. The others decay by emitting either alpha particles (as defined above), or beta particles (equivalent to electrons), or positrons (electrons with positive charge), or gamma rays (very short wavelength electromagnetic radiation).

The decay products (daughter products) may also be radioactive and will themselves decay further until stable nuclei are formed. Radioactivity can last a long time: the *half-lives* of most natural radioactive elements are measured in thousands of years (e.g. carbon-14) to billions (10^9) of years (e.g. uranium-238) (see Box 'Radioactive half-lives').

Radioactive half-lives

An impression of how quickly a radioactive isotope decays can be obtained from its **half-life**, which is the time it takes for half the total number of atoms to undergo a nuclear transformation (Figure 3). We saw earlier that half-lives of many radioactive elements are measurable in thousands to billions of years. For such long periods of time a convenient unit is Ma, representing one million (10^6) years, where 'a' is the SI symbol for year (being short for *annum*).

For uranium-235 the half-life is 704 Ma, meaning that half the original atoms will have decayed in this time, three-quarters in 1408 Ma, seven-eighths in 2112 Ma, and so on. For uranium-238 the half-life is 4468 Ma — so the Earth (which is about 4600 Ma old) has lost a much greater fraction of its uranium-235 than its uranium-238 atoms since it formed.

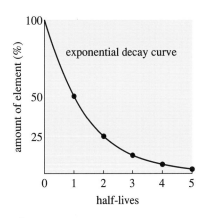

Figure 3 The concept of half-life, which leads to exponential decrease (decay) of (in this case) a radioactive element.

The energy produced by this natural radioactive decay is the *kinetic energy* of the emitted particles, which is converted into *thermal energy* (heat) when they collide with other nuclei. The heat produced by natural decay of radioactive elements that are dispersed in low concentrations in the Earth's outer layers (crust and mantle), is the cause of the Earth's internal heat. This heat is indirectly tapped when we exploit geothermal power (see Section 3). It is far too 'dilute' a source of energy to exploit directly for electricity generation, as the following Question illustrates.

Question 1

The rate of heat production by natural radioactive decay of uranium-238 is $3000 \, \text{J} \, \text{kg}^{-1} \, \text{y}^{-1}$. Roughly how long would it take for 1 kg of uranium to produce the same amount of energy as is contained in 1 kg of coal, which is $2.8 \times 10^7 \, \text{J}$?

So, radioactive decay cannot be used to fuel power stations. The property of nuclear *fission* is what makes uranium a concentrated energy source — but only after some technological intervention.

We saw earlier that natural fission of uranium nuclei occurs much less frequently than the emission of alpha particles by radioactive decay. In fact, in its natural state uranium-238 undergoes one fission for roughly every million radioactive alpha decays. To make nuclear fission a viable energy source, the fission rate must be greatly increased; but before describing how this is done, we need to understand a little more about the two isotopes uranium-235 and uranium-238.

All natural uranium consists of 99.3% uranium-238 and 0.7% uranium-235. The proportions were more evenly balanced early in the Earth's history, but the relative amount of uranium-235 decreased because its half-life is nearly ten times (an order of magnitude) shorter than that of uranium-238.

Despite its much lower abundance, however, uranium-235 is the isotope which provides the fissionable fuel in nuclear reactions. Here is how it works.

In a nuclear reactor, uranium atoms are bombarded with neutrons; this encourages them to release their stored energy much more rapidly, by increasing the rate of fission. The reaction, which forms the basis of virtually all existing nuclear power generating plants, involves the capture of low energy neutrons, called **slow neutrons**, by nuclei of the less common isotope uranium-235. This capture of slow neutrons increases the mass number of uranium-235 by one unit, producing $^{236}_{92}\text{U}$:

$$^{236}_{92}\text{U} + ^{1}_{0}\text{n} \rightarrow \, ^{236}_{92}\text{U} \tag{2.1}$$

This isotope is highly unstable and breaks down by fission, releasing energy in the way outlined above:

$$^{236}_{92}\text{U} \rightarrow \, ^{93}_{38}\text{Sr} + ^{140}_{54}\text{Xe} + 3^{1}_{0}\text{n} + 3.2 \times 10^{-11} \, \text{J} \tag{2.2}$$

typical fission   neutrons   energy
products

There are three important things to note about this reaction.

1 Although in *numerical* terms, the mass numbers and the atomic numbers total the same on both sides of Equation 2.2 (93 + 140 + 3 = 236, and 38 + 54 + 0 = 92), in *mass* terms, the sum of the parts (on the right) does not

quite equal the whole (on the left). There has been a small mass loss in the fission, and this has been converted to energy according to $E = mc^2$.

2   The main fission products (strontium-93 and xenon-140) are radioactive and will themselves decay to stable daughter products, releasing thermal energy in the process.

3   More neutrons are produced — three for every atom of uranium-236 that undergoes fission. (Note also that Equation 2.2 is just *one* example of uranium-236 fission. There are several other reactions but they all yield fission products with atomic numbers clustering around 90 and 140, along with two or three neutrons per fission).

⬤   What will happen if these neutrons collide with more nuclei of uranium-235?

◯   The reaction will continue, producing still more neutrons and more energy in an uncontrolled **chain reaction**, of the kind that occurs in atomic bombs, unless it is controlled in some way, as in a power station.

Equations 2.1 and 2.2 allow us to calculate the amount of energy produced by uncontrolled fission, known as the **fission energy** of uranium. It turns out that 1 kg of uranium-235 contains 25.5×10^{23} atoms. The fission energy available from one atom of uranium-235 (after conversion to uranium-236 and subsequent fission) is 3.2×10^{-11} J (Equation 2.2). So the amount of fission energy available from 1 kg of uranium-235 will be:

$$(25.5 \times 10^{23} \text{ atoms}) \times (3.2 \times 10^{-11} \text{ J per atom}) \approx 8.2 \times 10^{13} \text{ J}$$

Moles and Avogadro's constant

Here is how the figure of 25.5×10^{23} atoms per kg of uranium-235 is arrived at. A *mole* of any element will always contain the same number of atoms, 6×10^{23}, known as Avogadro's number or *Avogadro's constant*. A mole of any element can also be defined as the mass number of that element (its *relative atomic mass*) expressed in grams.

Thus, a mole of uranium-235 contains 6×10^{23} atoms and has a mass of 235 g. So, 1 kg (1000 g) of uranium-235 contains 1000/235 = 4.25 moles.

Which means that 1 kg of uranium-235 contains $4.25 \times 6 \times 10^{23} = 25.5 \times 10^{23}$ atoms.

Several points follow from our calculation of the fission energy of uranium-235:

1   The fission of 1 kg of uranium-235 produces about 3×10^{10} times more energy (8.2×10^{13} J/3×10^3 J) than is produced in one year by 1 kg of uranium-238 undergoing radioactive decay. Of course, fission energy per unit mass is not very different in *total* from that which is ultimately released by radioactive decay — it is merely released very rapidly instead of over the hundreds to thousands of millions of years it takes for the natural radioactive decay of uranium.

2   The fission energy from 1 kg of uranium-235 produces 8.2×10^{13}/$2.8 \times 10^7 \approx 3 \times 10^6$ times more energy than is obtained from 1 kg of coal. In other words, weight for weight, uranium-235 is three million times more concentrated than coal as an energy source. Also, although weight for weight it costs more than coal to mine, process and transport to the power station, its energy content is so high that it is a cheaper fuel than coal.

3   As we saw earlier, natural uranium contains much less uranium-235 than uranium-238 — 0.7% as against 99.3%. This means that only 0.7% of the fission energy calculated above will be obtained by the reactions in Equations 2.1 and 2.2 from a 1 kg block of natural uranium.

⬤   So why not exploit fission energy from the much more abundant isotope, uranium-238?

○   The principal reason is that uranium-238 is a more stable nucleus than uranium-235, and it does not capture slow neutrons (they just 'bounce off'). Only high-energy **fast neutrons** can penetrate the nucleus to be captured, transforming it to uranium-239, which in turn is converted (transmuted) first to neptunium-239 and then to plutonium-239:

$$^{238}_{92}\text{U} + ^{1}_{0}\text{n} \rightarrow ^{239}_{92}\text{U} \rightarrow ^{239}_{93}\text{Np} \rightarrow ^{239}_{94}\text{Pu} \tag{2.3}$$

The conversion (transmutation) to neptunium-239 and then to plutonium-239 occurs by rapid radioactive decay involving the emission of *beta particles* (electrons). As electrons carry a negative charge, beta-decay has the effect of removing a negative charge from a neutron, leaving a positively charged proton. Accordingly, while the mass number remains the same (239), the atomic number increases (from 92 to 94, for two beta particle emissions). Plutonium-239 is unstable and undergoes fission, releasing more neutrons and an amount of energy similar to that in Equation 2.2. Clearly, by exploiting the more abundant uranium isotope in this way, the potential of naturally occurring uranium as an energy resource can be increased by almost 150 times (100/0.7) compared with the energy extractable from uranium-235 alone. However, to establish an efficient chain reaction based on uranium-238 requires a supply of fast neutrons, and this involves much more advanced and complex technology, as we will see in Section 2.1.2.

Before moving on, however, we should clarify some outstanding points. We established earlier that fission of natural uranium occurs very infrequently (once for every million or so alpha decays) but it is not clear why it should occur at all. Where do the necessary neutrons come from? There must be some natural source of neutrons to get things started — and so there is. Alpha particles from ordinary radioactive decay can interact with nearby nuclei of other elements with high mass numbers (such as lead, itself a daughter product of radioactive uranium decay), and this sometimes 'knocks out' neutrons. Another way of generating neutrons is for beta particles, which carry a negative charge, to neutralize the positive charges on protons.

Once neutrons are available to set the initial reaction off, other neutrons will be generated by fission of the unstable uranium nuclei.

⬤   So, if more neutrons are generated by each fission, why does natural fission occur only infrequently? Why haven't natural chain reactions caused all uranium ores to self-destruct by fission long ago?

○   The surrounding rock absorbs nearly all the energy of the neutrons, the great majority of which rapidly lose their momentum in collisions with nuclei of other elements that are mostly neither fissionable nor radioactive. In other words, even in the richest ores the concentration of uranium is nothing like enough to keep a chain reaction going. Neutrons with a wide range of energies from high (fast) to low (slow) are generated in these 'natural' fission processes of both uranium-235 and uranium-238; but the moderating effect of the surrounding rock probably ensures that slow neutrons predominate. However, natural uranium contains only 0.7% uranium-235 as against 99.3% uranium-238. Slow neutrons have a 0.7 in 99.3 chance (roughly 1 in 150) of encountering a nucleus of uranium-235 rather than one of uranium-238, so the rate at which fission of uranium atoms occurs in the natural state may well be similar for both isotopes. Only one example of natural fission has been found so far (see Box 'A case of natural nuclear fission' in Section 2.1.2).

Having understood the basic principles of nuclear fission, we are now in a better position to see how fission energy is converted to heat energy to raise steam for electrical power generation. That is the subject of the next Section.

2.1.2 Nuclear reactors

For nuclear chain reactions (Equations 2.1 to 2.3) to take place, whether in an atomic bomb or in a nuclear reactor, a **critical mass** of uranium is necessary. Any lump of uranium smaller than the critical mass is not in danger of spontaneous fission; only when it is brought together with another lump sufficient to make up the critical mass can fission occur. In nuclear reactors, there *is* a critical mass of uranium, but the chain reaction is controlled by slowing down neutrons and absorbing any excess above those needed to keep the reaction going at the required rate.

The overwhelming majority of nuclear reactors make use of the reaction in Equation 2.2. They are called *burner reactors*.

Burner reactors

Here the main fuel is uranium-235 and the object is to use up or 'burn' as much of it as possible. Natural uranium contains only 0.7% uranium-235, so it is converted to **enriched uranium**, containing up to 3% uranium-235, to increase the efficiency of some types of burner reactor (Plate 40). The chain reactions in Equations 2.1 to 2.3 result in neutrons with a wide range of energies. Fast neutrons are slowed down using a **moderator** (so that they can cause fission of uranium-235) and the reaction rate is adjusted using **control rods** that totally absorb neutrons. The rods can be raised or lowered to increase or decrease the heat output. The moderator may be graphite or ordinary water (*light water*) or *heavy water* (deuterium oxide, $^2_1\text{H}_2\text{O}$; see Section 5.2) whilst the control rods are usually made of boron. Even in this type of reactor, some fast neutrons are absorbed by uranium-238 in the fuel rods to produce plutonium-239, nuclei of which then undergo fission and add appreciably to the total energy released. But the amount of plutonium created is much less than the amount of uranium used up and this is another reason why such reactors are called 'burner reactors'. (They are also called thermal reactors, because the slow neutrons which cause most of the fission of uranium-235 are technically termed thermal neutrons).

Figure 4 shows the essential design features of the three most common types of burner reactor in use today. They have certain features in common. They all have **cores** encased in steel vessels surrounded by concrete shields, and, as with fossil fuel power stations, the heat generated is used to convert water into steam; this is then directed under pressure into the generator turbines, after which it is condensed and returned to the boilers (see Figure 2 and inset of Figure 4). Whereas in fossil fuel stations the hot gaseous combustion products of coal or gas heat the water in the boilers directly, in nuclear power stations there is no combustion, and heat is transmitted to the boilers by a coolant fluid in a closed circuit between the boilers and the hot reactor core.

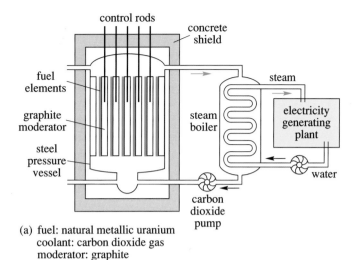

(a) fuel: natural metallic uranium
    coolant: carbon dioxide gas
    moderator: graphite

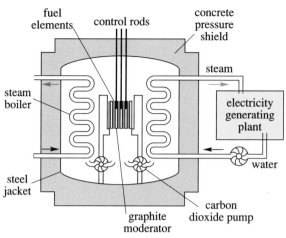

(b) fuel: slightly enriched uranium oxide
    coolant: carbon dioxide gas
    moderator: graphite

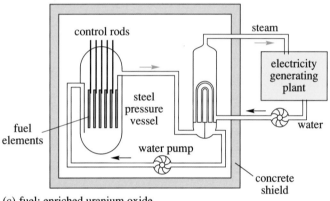

(c) fuel: enriched uranium oxide
    coolant: water
    moderator: water

The main contrasts between the three main burner reactor types are summarized below.

Magnox reactors (Figure 4a) are fuelled by metallic uranium containing the natural proportion of uranium-235 (i.e. 0.7%) held in tubes of a magnesium alloy (Magnox). The moderator is graphite, the coolant is carbon dioxide and the operating temperature is about 400 °C.

Advanced gas-cooled reactors (AGRs; Figure 4b) are very similar to Magnox reactors, except that uranium oxide, enriched in uranium-235 (2.3% instead of 0.7%) and packed in stainless steel tubes, is used as a fuel. The moderator and coolant are as in Magnox reactors but the operating temperature, 800 °C, is higher, leading to greater conversion efficiency and output. Although the capital cost of building AGRs is very high, they have many additional safety features over Magnox reactors and, because of their greater efficiency, produce cheaper electricity.

Pressurized water reactors (PWRs; Figure 4c) were only recently adopted in Britain (see Section 2.1.4) but are the most popular type worldwide. The fuel is uranium oxide, enriched in uranium-235 (up to 3%) and contained in zirconium alloy tubes, and pressurized light water is both coolant and moderator. They operate at 300–400 °C.

Burner reactors use uranium-235 which can be enriched to as much as 3% in the fuel rods or elements (see Section 2.3.2). So even the most enriched reactor fuel still consists of 97% of uranium-238. A very small proportion of this is converted to plutonium-239 (Equation 2.3), which provides a small additional increment of fission energy, but the bulk of the uranium in burner reactor fuel rods is never used. Indeed, the wastage is even greater than that:

Figure 4 Essential features of (a) a Magnox reactor, (b) an advanced gas-cooled reactor and (c) a pressurized water reactor. Diagram at lower right expands the boxes shown for a conventional steam turbine electricity generating plant, and is the same as Figure 2.

only about 0.5 to 2% of a uranium fuel rod is converted to useful energy because by no means all of the uranium-235 is 'burned', owing to the build-up of fission products which interfere with the chain reaction.

So why not develop reactors designed especially to extract fission energy from the much more abundant isotope, uranium-238?

Why not, indeed? If fast neutrons produced in the chain reactions in Equations 2.1 to 2.3 are not moderated (i.e. slowed down) or absorbed, the rate of conversion of uranium-238 into plutonium-239 can actually be made to *exceed* the fission rate of plutonium-239. Reactors using fast neutrons to create more plutonium-239 fuel than they use are called fast breeder reactors.

Fast breeder reactors

Here the main fuel is uranium-238, together with an initial charge of plutonium-239; this is needed to set in progress the chain reaction which uses fast neutrons to 'breed' plutonium-239 from uranium-238 continuously during the lifetime of the reactor. The initial charge may be extracted from the spent fuel rods of burner reactors or — and herein lies the attraction of this concept — from the excess plutonium-239 produced in fast breeders themselves (where the rate of plutonium production exceeds its rate of fission). In practice, about 60% of the fuel elements in breeder reactors can be converted into useful energy, compared with the 0.5–2% in burner reactors. Breeder reactors use uranium fuel much more efficiently than burners, and indeed the breeder process looks very much like getting something for nothing: fast breeders could greatly extend the lifetime of nuclear fuel reserves.

It seems very attractive, but the fact is that only a handful of fast breeders have ever been constructed, and Britain's own fast breeder programme was terminated in 1992 after some £4 billion had been spent over four decades in research and development, with only the 250 MW prototype fast breeder reactor at Dounreay in Scotland (Figure 5) to show for it — and that was finally closed down in 1994. There is only one fast breeder left in the USA, and it was due to close before the end of the decade. Operational problems forced closure of the French fast breeder (Superphénix) in 1990, though it came back on stream in 1994, despite some public opposition. Elsewhere, only Japan appears to be continuing with a fast breeder programme.

Figure 5   The Dounreay prototype fast breeder reactor on the north Scottish coast, which began operating in 1975 (foreground); the experimental fast breeder core, built in 1959, lies within the white dome in the background. It was decommissioned in 1977.

All of this testifies to formidable problems with fast breeder technology; the main trouble is that fast neutrons have high kinetic energy and produce a great deal of heat when they collide with atomic nuclei. The intense heat generated by the fast-neutron chain reaction requires the circulation of highly conductive liquid sodium as the coolant (Figure 6), and it is this aspect that presents the main technical problem, especially as the operating temperature is around 600 °C. Moreover, the efficient operation of the breeder reactor also requires a 'density' of fast neutrons much higher than the 'density' of slow neutrons required in burner reactors. The neutrons emerging from the chain reaction must not make collisions that would slow them down before they strike uranium-238 nuclei; hence the core region of a fast breeder, besides containing no moderator, must be more compact than that of a burner reactor, and it must contain only the minimum volume of coolant. Despite these difficulties, however, it would be a mistake to suppose that fast breeder technology will never have a future.

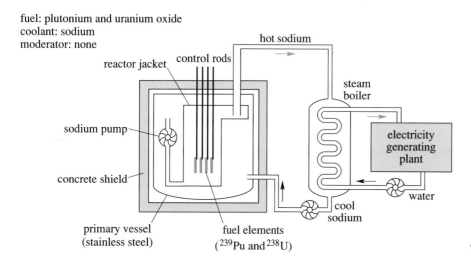

fuel: plutonium and uranium oxide
coolant: sodium
moderator: none

Figure 6 Essential features of a fast breeder reactor.

A case of natural nuclear fission

In Section 2.1.1 we saw that the half-life of uranium-235 is shorter than that of uranium-238, so that in the past the proportion of uranium-235 in natural uranium was greater than it is now. Uranium ores at Oklo in Gabon (West Africa) are 1800 Ma (million years) old, and would have contained about 3% of uranium-235 at the time of their formation (the same as the enriched fuel used in PWRs). Moreover, the percentage of uranium in the ores rises locally to 50%, very much richer than in most ores (see Section 2.2.1) and enough to provide a critical mass in several places. The ores would have lain beneath the water table and so would have been saturated with water, which would have acted as moderator for fast neutrons. Chain reactions could have been initiated by neutrons produced from the spontaneous fission of uranium-235. These natural reactors ran for several thousand years, during which time they generated an estimated 100×10^9 kWh of energy, the same as a modern nuclear reactor running for about 5 years.

How was this discovered? During a routine French laboratory testing of uranium hexafluoride derived from Oklo uranium ore, it was found that some samples had uranium-235 concentrations less than the normal 0.7% in natural uranium. The only way in which this could be explained was if the uranium-235 had been used up in a fission chain reaction. Subsequent investigation of the mines from which the samples came confirmed this hypothesis, through analysis of the fission products present in the ore.

The occurrence of this example of natural fission reactors would be of theoretical interest only, were it not for the information it provides about the dispersal of radioactive waste products from fission reactors, a topic we address in Section 2.3.3.

2.1.3 Fuel requirements for nuclear reactors

Earlier, we showed that the fission energy of uranium-235 is 8.2×10^{13} J per kilogram. To put this figure into the context of fuelling a reactor, we need to consider:

1 *The thermal efficiency of the reactor*   For modern burner reactors, this is similar to that of modern fossil fuel power stations, about 35% (i.e. 65% of the available energy is lost within the reactor–coolant–turbine system).

2 *The power output*   A typical value for a burner reactor is 1000 MW (= 1 GW) which corresponds to an annual energy output of 3.2×10^{16} J y^{-1}.

3 *The lifetime of the reactor*   This may be 30 years, i.e. of about the same order as for conventional fossil fuel power stations.

Fuel elements (rods) do not last for 30 years, and the total fuel requirement for a typical 1 GW burner reactor is about 4800 tonnes of natural uranium over a 30-year period. Some 600 tonnes of natural uranium is required as an initial fuelling charge (less if the fuel has been enriched in uranium-235); and an average of about 145 tonnes per year is used to replace spent fuel rods. Even where fuel enriched in uranium-235 has been used, spent fuel rods comprise some 96% of **depleted uranium**, which has lost most of its uranium-235 component, and is therefore mainly uranium-238, along with less than 1% of plutonium-239 (up to 50 tonnes total — depending on reactor characteristics — after 30 years), both of which are potentially available for a fast breeder reactor cycle (see below). The remaining 2–3% of spent fuel rods is composed mainly of fission products. The fuel requirements and products of burner reactors are summarized in Figure 7a.

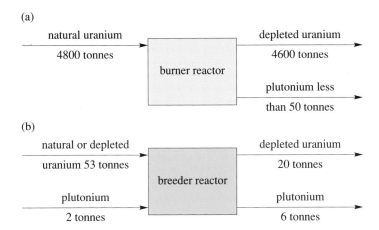

Figure 7   A summary of the fuel requirements and spent fuel products from (a) a typical burner reactor and (b) a fast breeder reactor, based, in both cases, on a power output of 1000 MW for 30 years.

The fact that less than 5000 tonnes of natural uranium (containing 0.7% uranium-235) is needed to fuel a 1000 MW burner reactor over a 30-year lifetime, provides a powerful illustration of the 'energy density' of uranium relative to fossil fuels. A modern coal-fired power station of comparable output needs to burn something like 10 000 tonnes of coal *per day*. The total volume of waste to be disposed of during the life of a power station is thus also much less for nuclear than for coal.

When it comes to fast breeder reactors, the comparison is starker still. In this case, the fuel consists of uranium-238, whose fission energy (8.6×10^{13} J kg^{-1}) is slightly more than that of uranium-235 (8.2×10^{13} J kg^{-1}), but the difference is that about 60% of the fuel is used. This means that a 35% efficient 1000 MW fast breeder reactor would need a little over 50 tonnes of natural uranium during its 30-year lifetime, i.e. about *100 times less* than the fuel requirement of an equivalent burner reactor.

If you were not convinced before, this should really emphasize the point that burner reactors are extravagantly wasteful of nuclear fuel — unless the depleted uranium can be reprocessed and used later in a breeder reactor. Moreover, although the fast breeder reactor requires an initial charge of about 2 tonnes of plutonium-239 to get going (Equation 2.3), after 30 years there will be *more* plutonium-239 in the fuel rods than is invested in the initial charge (Figure 7b). Unlike burner reactors which must be periodically supplied with fresh fuel rods during their active life, a successful breeder reactor would require relatively little attention once it had received its initial charge. Figure 8 illustrates the annual supply of fuel required to service 1000 MW (= 1 GW) power stations using coal, burner and breeder technologies once they are in production.

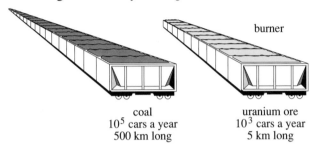

burner   breeder

coal
10^5 cars a year
500 km long

uranium ore
10^3 cars a year
5 km long

uranium ore
zero cars a year

Figure 8 The annual coal and uranium ore requirements for different kinds of 1000 MW power station. (An average grade of 0.3% uranium in the uranium ore was assumed for this Figure.)

2.1.4 The growth of nuclear power

The origins of the nuclear industry go back to the discovery of fission in 1939. During the later years of the Second World War (1939–45) much scientific effort was expended in the USA on the military uses of nuclear energy, culminating in the Hiroshima atomic bomb.

The UK's first commercial power station, a Magnox reactor, was opened at Calder Hall (Figure 9) in 1956. By the late 1950s the UK was at the forefront of world nuclear developments with six commercial reactors operating, and the successful exportation of Magnox technology to Italy and Japan. The UK Magnox reactor building programme was complete in 1971 with eight stations, each producing between 245 MW and 840 MW (Plate 41).

The newer AGRs were designed to use enriched uranium fuel and higher operating temperatures, thus increasing power output efficiency from 30% to a maximum of 40%. After a long history of technical difficulties and delays, eight 1000 MW AGR reactors, originally designed and planned in the early 1970s, are now in service.

However, the American-designed PWRs became by far the most attractive reactor design elsewhere. Some 240 PWRs are operating successfully worldwide, leaving only the UK with AGR stations. But PWRs have not been without their problems (see Box on 'PWR safety').

Despite their proliferation, concerns over the operational safety of PWRs dramatically slowed the world growth rate of nuclear power during the 1980s. US utility companies had stopped ordering reactors by 1978, even before the Three Mile Island incident, because of concern about the relative economics of nuclear and fossil fuel stations. Similar worries in Europe were exacerbated by a serious reactor accident in 1986 at Chernobyl in Ukraine (Section 2.3.1), and by 1990 world nuclear developments had virtually come to a halt everywhere except in France and Japan.

It is interesting that France commenced its nuclear energy programme well behind most other countries, including the USA and UK, yet its combined nuclear and hydropower resources now allow the exportation of some 10% of the electricity generated. So why has France been so successful in avoiding the political, environmental and economic constraints affecting

PWR safety

In the early 1970s, about 1% of the zirconium-clad fuel rods leaked, releasing fission product gases to the cooling water. However, by 1992 fuel fabrication had improved; for example, General Electric Co. in the USA claimed that of the last 433 000 fuel rods they made, only two had leaked.

Another aspect of PWRs is that the fuel rods are packed into a much smaller reactor core than in AGRs: the fuel is about 40 times more densely packed. So if the (pressurized) PWR cooling system were to fail, the reactor core would heat up to danger level much more rapidly than in an AGR. Indeed, PWRs came under serious criticism following the Three Mile Island incident in Pennsylvania during 1979, when safe-guard mechanisms failed to prevent a serious increase in the temperature and pressure of the reactor core, followed by a leak of radioactive materials. The reactor developed a gas bubble in its core, increasing the danger of a further rise in temperature and ultimately a 'meltdown' which would result in the melting of the reactor core containment vessel. Although some subsequent reports have indicated that the damage arose from a combination of technical and operator failures which are unlikely to be repeated, rather than from fundamental design weaknesses, there is still considerable public opposition to PWRs.

attitudes in most other countries? Doubtless, the centralized government and state-owned electricity company (EDF) have allowed a clear national policy to be developed and marketed attractively. Incentives in the form of reduced electricity prices are provided to populations in the vicinity of new nuclear stations. There is also economic strength in being strongly committed to a particular programme; for example, Britain's first PWR (see below) cost £2 billion compared with £0.9 billion for a French PWR of similar capacity. Of more questionable importance to French attitudes is the fact that one of the Second World War heroes of the left-wing opposition, Frédérick Joliot, was a pioneer and proponent of nuclear energy. So, despite the large reputed debts of EDF, it is not surprising that French citizens are proud of their nuclear programme, which includes commercial fast breeders. In the early 1990s eight new nuclear stations were under construction in France with five more at an advanced stage of planning; while in the UK just one nuclear station was under construction, at Sizewell on the Suffolk coast (Sizewell B, Figure 9). Sizewell B is the sole survivor of ten PWRs that were planned in the early 1980s to benefit from foreign PWR experience, and was commissioned in 1995.

The Sizewell B proposal developed into one of the most protracted public enquiries on record, lasting 333 days across 1983–85. Objectors argued that a further nuclear station would not be required on the proposed timescale (commissioning in the mid-1990s), that the PWR safety record was suspect, and that the full cost of nuclear power had never been properly assessed. The crux of the then CEGB (Central Electricity

Figure 9 Locations of the most important nuclear sites and power stations in Britain as of 1994. Reprocessing of spent nuclear fuels and waste disposal are considered in Section 2.3.2.

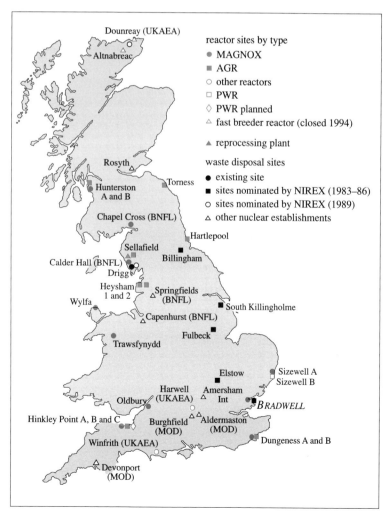

Figure 10 Britain's first pressurized water reactor (Sizewell B, see Figure 9) under construction in July 1991. The dome being lifted onto the reactor roof is bigger than that of St Paul's Cathedral.

Generating Board) argument lay in proving that the design and safety targets for a British PWR would be acceptable and that nuclear power is cheaper to produce than fossil fuel power, a claim that proved difficult to justify, as we shall see. In the event, although permission was granted for the Sizewell B PWR to be built (Figure 10), the enquiry debate successfully exposed the financial problems of the nuclear industry.

Although a second major planning enquiry (1988–89) approved the building of a second PWR at Hinkley Point (Station C; Figure 9), the Government decided, in planning for electricity privatization in 1990: (a) to maintain the old Magnox stations and the AGRs in public ownership, and (b) to abandon the full PWR construction programme. The future of Hinkley Point C thus remains in doubt.

Worries about the cost of nuclear power may well have influenced these decisions: £15 billion had so far been spent in constructing nuclear stations, and the price for decommissioning reactors and managing waste is still unknown. Ignoring the latter costs, in 1992 most estimates placed the cost of nuclear power (about 5.5p per unit) rather higher than for fossil fuel stations (3.9–4.5p per unit at a time when the average domestic unit price was 7.5p). It was argued that fossil fuel generators should pay a carbon tax commensurate with their emission of the greenhouse gas CO_2, which would have made costs more comparable. Nevertheless, during the run-up to the electricity industry privatization, the City quickly reached the commercial conclusion that the nuclear power sector was not saleable. Instead, public ownership was transferred for generation to Nuclear Electric (England and Wales) and Scottish Nuclear (Scotland), while British Nuclear Fuels (BNFL) continued to represent the UK's interest in fuel supply and reprocessing.

Nuclear electricity is reasonably competitive in the UK, partly because of the Non-Fossil Fuel Obligation, introduced at the time of electricity privatization, which requires electricity companies to purchase all the output from nuclear and alternative energy sources. More important, the nuclear generators receive a £1.2 billion annual government subsidy, estimated to be worth 2–3p per kWh and paid for, at least in part, by the 'nuclear levy', a 10% surcharge on all electricity bills. However, Nuclear Electric and Scottish Nuclear were claiming in 1993 that they might be able to dispense with this subsidy by the end of the decade, in the light of actual and anticipated profits which they hoped might also make the industry more attractive to private investors — indeed, during 1994 Nuclear Electric began campaigning actively for privatization, and had obtained government support by mid-1995. The question is, would private investors be required (or prepared) to bear all or part of the financial burden of decommissioning reactors at the end of their useful lives? The 'nuclear levy' was introduced to help pay for decommissioning, but the total cost of this operation is still enormous: it has been variously quoted as £16–18 billion, £26 billion, and even £40 billion.

The sheer scale of the decommissioning problem can be illustrated by the nuclear industry's own argument that 'costs will be considerably reduced' if the closure and decommissioning timetable is spread over 135 years instead of 100 years, and if reactor cores and pressure vessels are not dismantled but buried instead. This is what was done at the Berkeley Magnox station in Gloucestershire (near the Oldbury site; Figure 9), which closed in 1989. In 1992 the Hunterston A Magnox station near Glasgow ceased generating elecricity, and in 1993 Nuclear Electric announced the closure of the Trawsfynydd Magnox station in Snowdonia (Plate 42), which had been idle for two years because of technical faults, and estimated its decommissioning costs at £600 million over 100 years. At the same time the company sought clearance to extend the life of its six remaining Magnox reactors for another 30 years.

The international scene

By the mid-1990s the future of nuclear power in the USA and most of Western Europe (France excluded) was economically and politically uncertain, even though the industry itself was strong scientifically and its technology still improving. On the other hand, in France, Japan and other countries of the Pacific Rim (Table 1), the high level of science and the improving technology was matched by a bright economic scene and a favourable political situation. In the former Soviet Republics and Eastern Europe, where scientific and technical developments have lagged somewhat behind those in the West, the economic and political picture was less clear. But this is potentially a very lucrative market and by 1993 nuclear industries in several Western countries, faced with declining business at home, had begun competing vigorously to acquire a share of it.

Against this background, forecasts of future requirements for nuclear-generated electricity should be viewed with caution. Thus, the OECD (Organization for Economic Co-operation and Development) estimated in 1990 that world nuclear electricity generating capacity would rise from 318 GW (1990) to 368 GW in 2005 and perhaps to 600 GW by 2030 as a result of legislation aimed at reducing greenhouse gas emissions. In contrast, estimates by the International Atomic Energy Agency (IAEA) in 1991 suggested that nuclear generating capacity worldwide in 2005 might not significantly exceed the 1990 figure of about 320 GW and could even be less than that.

Which of these estimates proves to be nearer the truth must depend on factors such as: (a) the extent to which society's demand for electricity continues to grow; (b) public perception of the dangers and costs of nuclear power generation; (c) whether governments perceive the threat of global warming as real enough to warrant serious attempts at curbing greenhouse gas emissions from fossil fuels; and (d) the extent to which alternative energy sources can meet society's needs. At all events, nuclear fuels continue to be needed, and we now turn to how this need can be met.

2.2 Uranium: reserves, resources and lifetime

The next stage is to consider uranium resources and to enquire what restriction their availability and price may impose on nuclear power generation. We shall start with a brief overview of uranium geology to set the scene. As you read on, you need to bear in mind an important point about mining uranium ores (or any other ores). The caption to Figure 8 noted that the estimated number of 'ore trucks' for nuclear reactors is based on an ore containing 0.3% of uranium, that is, with a **grade** of 0.3%. A 1 GW (1000 MW) burner reactor needs about 5000 tonnes of natural uranium over its lifetime of 30 years. The tonnage of ore containing 0.3% uranium that must be mined to produce this amount of uranium is close to 1.7 million tonnes.

Question 2

What tonnage of waste will be left after that ore has been processed to remove its uranium? Give your answer to two significant figures.

2.2.1 Uranium geology

Uranium is an element that occurs mainly as an oxide mineral, typically U_3O_8, known as *uraninite* (and when black and massive, *pitchblende*). The average concentration of uranium in mantle peridotite is about 0.03 parts per million (p.p.m.), in basalts 1 p.p.m., and in granites 3.5 p.p.m. This suggests it is an element that is concentrated during partial melting and fractional crystallization events in the rock cycle. The upper continental crust contains, on average, 3 p.p.m. uranium.

⬤ For Question 2 we used an ore grade of 0.3%. By how much must uranium be concentrated above its average continental crustal concentration to form an ore of this grade?

◯ 0.3% is 0.3 parts in 100, written 0.3×10^{-2}, and 3 p.p.m. is 3 parts in one million (10^6), written 3×10^{-6}. The degree of concentration required is therefore:

$$\frac{0.3 \times 10^{-2}}{3 \times 10^{-6}} = \frac{3 \times 10^{-3}}{3 \times 10^{-6}} = 10^3 \text{ or } 1000 \text{ times}$$

Uranium ore deposits should contain upwards of 350 p.p.m. uranium (0.035%) before they can even be considered for profitable exploitation, though the minimum concentration, or **cut-off grade**, that can be mined at a profit is subject to local economic conditions and is commonly much higher than 350 p.p.m. But what processes form these uranium ores and what kinds of deposit are involved? The answer is not simple, for uranium occurs in a variety of settings, but the key to understanding the behaviour of uranium in the rock cycle is the fact that it forms large, highly charged ions: U^{4+}, ionic radius 97 picometres (pm = 10^{-12} m), and U^{6+}, 80 pm. Both are much larger than Si^{4+} (ionic radius 42 pm), the second most common element in the Earth's crust after oxygen, and both are more highly charged than most of the other common cations (e.g. Fe^{2+}, Mg^{2+}, Ca^{2+}, Na^+). For this reason uranium does not readily fit into the structures of the common silicate minerals (pyroxenes, feldspars, micas and so on) of which most rocks are composed.

Uranium is classed among the **incompatible elements**, and as such will always be among the last elements to crystallize from a cooling magma.

Among magmatic rocks, granites have the lowest temperatures of crystallization, and granitic magmas are products of partial melting or fractional crystallization into which incompatible elements are concentrated. That helps to explain why the average concentration of uranium is higher in granites and associated rocks than in other common igneous rocks such as basalt. The uranium is normally accommodated in accessory minerals with exotic names like monazite, pyrochlore, allanite; it will form minerals of its own (uraninite, pitchblende) only where its concentration is high enough. Under favourable conditions, uranium concentrations in granitic rocks can reach or even exceed the minimum cut-off grade of 350 p.p.m., occurring as uranium-rich minerals more or less evenly distributed through the rocks as **disseminated magmatic deposits**.

Like many other incompatible elements, uranium tends to dissolve more readily in heated groundwaters than do the common elements which fit easily into the structures of rock-forming minerals. Hot springs and geysers are present-day surface manifestations of **hydrothermal activity**, occurring in active volcanic regions and/or where a recently solidified (and therefore still hot) igneous intrusion lies at relatively shallow depth beneath the surface. Nearby groundwater is heated and rises towards the surface, drawing in cold groundwater towards the heat source — either through intergranular spaces (*primary permeability*) or through joints and cracks (*secondary permeability*) — to be heated and convected towards the surface in its turn. The convecting system is supplied by rainwater *infiltrating* the surrounding land surface over wide areas.

The heated groundwaters are a potential source of geothermal energy, as we will see in Section 3. They are also **hydrothermal solutions** which are commonly saline as well as hot and which have leached elements from the rocks through which they move — including the incompatible elements such as uranium which are not strongly bound in mineral structures. Hydrothermal systems extend through many cubic kilometres of crust and may persist for many thousands — perhaps even for millions — of years. Over the course of time, the solutions cool and crystallize in fissures or other spaces within the rocks, precipitating their dissolved load to form **hydrothermal vein deposits**, which may contain ores of valuable metals, including (in this case) uranium. A magmatic or volcanic heat source is not essential for hydrothermal activity — if groundwater can percolate deep enough into the crust, say along a fault system, it can be heated to high temperatures by the *geothermal gradient* alone (see Section 3), and then convect towards the surface again, perhaps along another fault system.

Uranium ores that occur in hydrothermal veins and igneous intrusions have been formed by internal Earth processes and are known as **primary uranium deposits**. There is often a close association between disseminated magmatic deposits and hydrothermal veins. Indeed, economic hydrothermal concentrations may represent remobilization (in aqueous solution) of uranium from deeper, subeconomic magmatic concentrations. Dissolution of dispersed uranium into hot, saline solutions convecting through a granite may be followed by upwards migration of those solutions through cracks, fissures and faults where they cool and redeposit the uranium in a more concentrated form. Veins containing massive pitchblende precipitated in the interstices between fragments of rock broken and crushed by movement along fault zones (*fault breccias*) are the typical product of such a process (Figure 11).

Some of the world's richest uranium deposits occur where rising hydrothermal solutions have been impeded by impermeable sedimentary

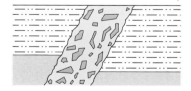

Figure 11 Uranium mineralization in veins may take place by precipitation from hydrothermal solution between the crushed and angular fragments of wall rock — the fault breccia — produced by movement along a fault zone.

rocks, which were deposited on an eroded surface of older rocks — an erosional *unconformity*. The impermeable sediments prevented the solutions from rising any further. They spread out and precipitated ore minerals where the rocks below the unconformity were most heavily faulted and brecciated, forming **vein-unconformity deposits** (Figure 12).

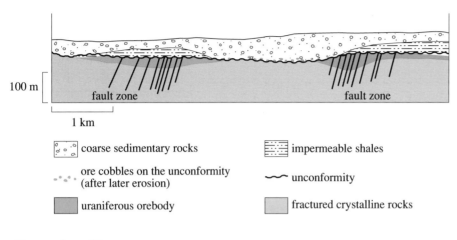

Figure 12 Cross-section of a vein-unconformity deposit. Mineralization has occurred where rising solutions have spread out beneath impermeable rocks unconformably covering the erosion surface. The coarse sedimentary rocks were deposited after a second erosional episode had distributed ore cobbles over the unconformity.

Question 3

To what extent are the physical factors controlling the location of hydrothermal vein-unconformity deposits analogous to those which govern the accumulation of hydrocarbons in oil and gas fields?

Uranium can also be concentrated by sedimentary processes to form **secondary uranium deposits**. The key to understanding the behaviour of uranium in sedimentary environments is simply that it occurs as the highly soluble U^{6+} ion under oxidizing conditions, and as the insoluble U^{4+} ion under reducing conditions. Thus uranium can be dissolved and transported by oxidizing ground waters but is deposited when reducing conditions are encountered.

Sandstone-hosted uranium deposits are a common type of secondary uranium deposit, and they are formed as follows. Imagine a sequence of shales and sandstones deposited as sediments derived in part by the erosion of a uranium-bearing granite. The sandstones formed under oxidizing conditions and are therefore unlikely to contain uranium minerals, because uranium is soluble in oxidizing environments. Most of the uranium from erosion of the granite will be dissolved in groundwater migrating through coarse permeable layers in the sedimentary sequence (Figure 13). However, where the sediments contain significant amounts of oxygen-demanding organic matter, the groundwaters become chemically reducing.

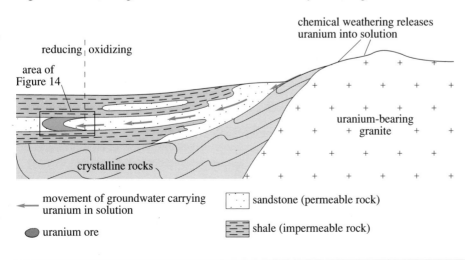

Figure 13 A cross-section illustrating the formation of uranium ore from groundwater and showing the relationship between mineralization and the oxidation state of the sandstone hosting the ore.

● What will happen to the dissolved uranium at this point?

○ At the boundary between oxidizing and reducing conditions, known as the **redox front**, uranium will be deposited to form secondary ore deposits. Often these take the form of a series of C- or S-shaped curved surfaces or 'ore fronts' ranging from 0.5 m to 10 m in vertical cross-section through a single sandstone bed (Figure 14; Plate 43) — hence the term **roll-type uranium ores**.

shale

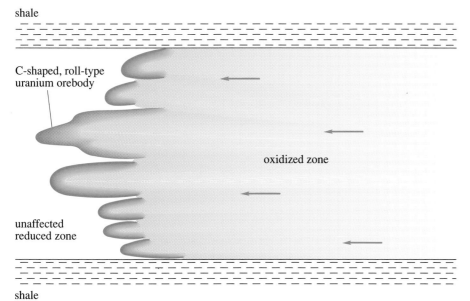

C-shaped, roll-type uranium orebody

oxidized zone

unaffected reduced zone

shale

Figure 14 Roll-type uranium ores produced by groundwater percolation (from right to left) in sandstone. Notice the sharp front edge of the roll produced at the oxidation–reduction boundary, and the diffuse rear edge in the oxidized zone.

These are typical of the sandstone-hosted uranium deposits formed in sedimentary basins that are surrounded by upland areas containing above-average uranium contents. Grades in these deposits range from about 0.1% to about 1%, and they may contain thousands to tens of thousands of tonnes of uranium as well lesser quantities of copper and vanadium ore minerals. Locally, whole tree trunks can be seen to have been replaced by the mineralizing solutions.

Uranium ores also occur in **quartz-pebble conglomerate deposits**, which contain uranium-bearing mineral particles deposited in fossilized river gravels in exactly the same form — principally uraninite — as when they were eroded from primary deposits.

● Under what conditions could uraninite grains be transported significant distances by surface waters?

○ This would happen if the Earth's atmosphere was non-oxidizing. There is abundant evidence from the geological record that until about 2000 Ma ago the atmosphere was only weakly oxidizing, so that uranium could be dissolved only slowly compared with today. So primary uraninite, a very dense mineral ($9000\,\text{kg m}^{-3}$), could have been transported by rivers and become concentrated in places where the speed of the water current decreased. The processes of cementation and lithification of the resulting sediments to form sedimentary rocks then preserved the uraninite grains from exposure to oxidizing groundwaters. Quartz-pebble conglomerate deposits of uranium cannot have formed later than about 2000 Ma ago, because after that the atmosphere became more strongly oxidizing and uranium would be soluble in surface waters — i.e. uraninite is unstable in the present-day surface weathering environment.

Finally, a few per cent of uranium resources are found in other sedimentary environments, notably in organic-rich sediments (e.g. black shales) of various geological ages, where reducing conditions prevailed during sedimentation in stagnant *anaerobic* environments, e.g. lagoons and coastal swamps. It should therefore not come as a surprise to learn that the Jurassic Kimmeridge Clay, which is the source rock for much of the oil in the North Sea, is also rich in uranium, while some coals can carry as much as 6000 p.p.m. of uranium, which is well above the minimum cut-off grade of 350 p.p.m. quoted earlier.

Uranium in the rock cycle

High concentrations of uranium can be achieved by a combination of magmatic, hydrothermal and surface processes in the rock cycle. Imagine a piece of ancient continental crust containing granites and undergoing weathering and erosion (Figure 15a). Uranium may become concentrated by a variety of surface processes into, say, shales and sandstones. Now suppose these sedimentary rocks become progressively buried beneath younger sedimentary rocks. Eventually they may undergo metamorphism (Figures 15b and 15c) and may reach high enough temperatures to start melting. In the same way that uranium is selectively concentrated in the last melts during crystallization processes, so it will tend to enter the first melts formed by partial melting. Thus, in the formation of a new generation of magmas that rise and intrude younger formations (Figure 15c), partial melting processes can selectively extract and enrich uranium in the magma. Repetition of this cycle over periods of tens of hundreds of millions of years can result in rocks with economic quantities of uranium.

Primary uranium deposits tend to occur in regions underlain by ancient continental shields, or **cratons**, which have been reactivated repeatedly by ancient plate tectonic processes leading to erosion–burial–metamorphism–

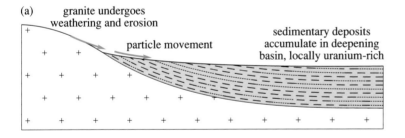

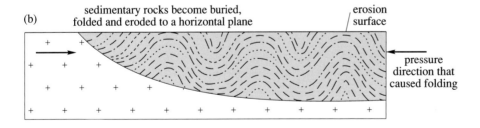

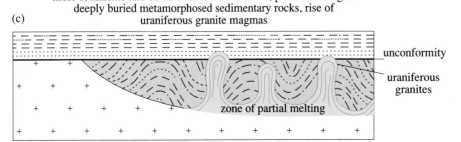

Figure 15 The sedimentary–metamorphic–igneous processes that may lead to a progressive concentration of crustal uranium to form ore deposits associated with uraniferous granites. But see also note in caption to Figure 17.

magmatism cycles as just described (Figure 15). It seems that the rate of crustal recycling and the surface conditions leading to uranium enrichment were particularly favourable during mid-Precambrian times. So we find economic concentrations of primary uranium (Figure 16a) in the cratons of North America (particularly Canada), Greenland and the Baltic area, Brazil, Southern Africa (Rossing) and Australia. Younger uraniferous granites (with associated hydrothermal vein deposits) occur throughout the Variscan province (about 300 Ma old) of southern and central Europe. Also shown on the map are major hydrothermal deposits, especially the vein–unconformity deposits of Key Lake (Canada) and Alligator Rivers (Australia).

The distribution of some important secondary uranium deposits is shown in Figure 16b, including sandstone-hosted uranium deposits of the Wyoming and Colorado areas of the American Mid-West, where they formed in sedimentary basins surrounded by upland areas containing above-average uranium concentrations. Also shown is the 2500 Ma old Witwatersrand basin of South Africa, containing probably the world's largest quartz-pebble conglomerate deposit of uranium, formed by erosion from one of the ancient cratons where primary uranium deposits are also found.

(a)

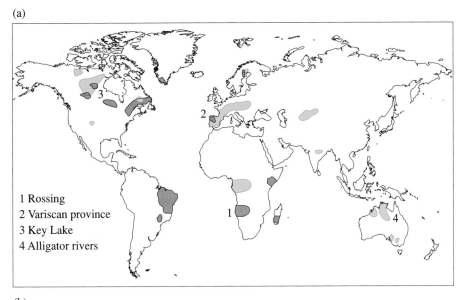

1 Rossing
2 Variscan province
3 Key Lake
4 Alligator rivers

(b)

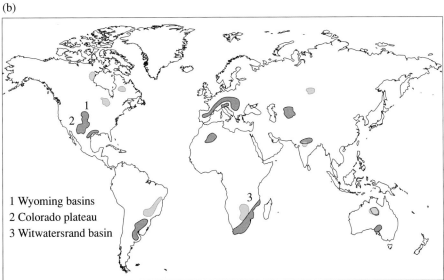

1 Wyoming basins
2 Colorado plateau
3 Witwatersrand basin

Figure 16 Location maps for the world's major uranium deposits. (a) Primary uranium directly associated with magmatic intrusions (grey) and with hydrothermal veins (colour). (b) Secondary uranium in sandstone-hosted deposits (grey) and quartz-pebble conglomerate deposits (colour).

A summary of the processes of formation of different kinds of uranium ore deposits is presented in Figure 17, and a summary of typical grades and sizes of the deposits reviewed in this Section is provided in Table 2.

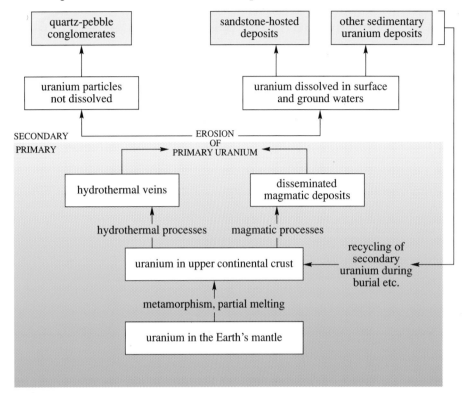

Figure 17 Uranium in the rock cycle, summarizing the sources of uranium and showing how it may be mobilized and concentrated into the main types of ore deposit in Table 2. Note that this is idealized, in that most uranium (and other elements) simply circulate round the rock cycle without becoming concentrated into ores. That is why ores are uncommon rocks.

Table 2 The main categories of uranium ore deposits

Type	Uranium grade (%)	Commonly associated metals	Largest known deposits (tonnes U)	Percentage of worldwide resources*
Primary				
disseminated magmatic	0.03–0.13	tin, tungsten	100 000	13
hydrothermal veins	0.1–4.0	molybdenum, nickel	200 000	25
Secondary				
sandstone-hosted	0.1–1.0	vanadium	40 000	37
quartz-pebble conglomerate	0.01–0.1	gold	15 000	16
others	0.3 (max)	various	various	9

* These are reasonably assured resources which in the uranium industry are classified as 'all the reserves and conditional resources priced at less than 130 US dollars per kilogram of uranium' (see Section 2.2.2).

2.2.2 Uranium production and economics

So far we have considered uranium as an energy resource and have looked at the geological processes that concentrate uranium naturally, to produce minable uranium ores. Once the ore has been mined either in surface open pits (e.g. most sandstone and disseminated deposits) or in deep underground mines (e.g. most vein deposits) it is taken to a mill. Here it is crushed and the uranium is leached into solution, leaving a massive amount of waste rock (*tailings*; see Box on 'Mine wastes') which must be disposed of, often by back-filling the mine. The solution is passed through *ion-exchange columns* that are capable of selectively extracting a particular element from solution, or releasing it into another solution, under different chemical conditions. The purified solution from ion exchange is treated with ammonia, and uranium is precipitated as an ammonium uranyl salt which is dried, roasted (heated in air) and shipped as **yellowcake**, an impure form of uranium trioxide (Figure 18).

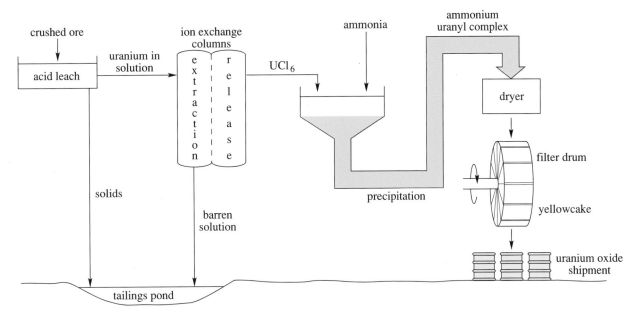

Figure 18 Simplified flow diagram showing the operation of a uranium mill. Uranium minerals are leached from the crushed ore in an acid bath and are then extracted from other acid-soluble material in ion exchange columns. Uranium is released as uranium chloride and then precipitated as an ammonium salt which is dried and roasted to produce 'yellowcake' oxide for shipment.

Mine wastes

Mine wastes (called *tailings*) always contain a certain amount of the ore being worked because no mining operation can hope to achieve 100% extraction of ore. The amount of waste produced is prodigious, especially where low-grade ores (like those of uranium) are involved (see Question 2). An ore grading of 0.5% uranium oxide is a rich ore, but for every tonne of uranium oxide extracted from it there are more than 200 tonnes of waste, much of it containing traces of uranium and possibly other radioactive elements. Uranium mining is no less demanding of water (for processing ore) than any other form of mineral extraction, and fine wastes from ore crushing and separation—whether from underground or surface operations—are pumped in suspension or as slurry to tailings dams. Dust blown by wind or washed by rain from dried-out tailings, dams and mine waste heaps can contaminate large areas of surrounding country unless steps are taken to prevent it happening. For example, after the demise of the former Soviet Union, it became apparent that uranium mining areas in the former eastern bloc (e.g. former East Germany) had higher than normal incidence of cancers, including lung cancer and childhood leukaemia, as well as various respiratory diseases. There are allegations that lax safety standards have led to similar consequences in other uranium mining areas (e.g. Australia, India, Namibia), but this is an emotive issue and allegations must be proved before they are accepted. Nowadays all mining companies are a great deal more safety conscious than they ever used to be.

Radon inhalation and other side-effects

There are hazardous side-effects for people working in the uranium industry in the form of **radon**, which is released by alpha decay of both uranium isotopes. This is a highly radioactive gas. It damages lung tissue after inhalation because it produces both α–particles and *solid* radioactive daughter products, particles of which can lodge in the lungs. The early uranium miners referred to the deteriorating lung condition which results as 'mountain sickness'. The risks are now minimized but not eliminated by the use of powerful ventilation, though this may not always be done in older mines or in less developed regions where the industrial risks are not fully appreciated.

In any case, much uranium mining is done in open-pit operations, where inhalation of radon gas is less of a problem, but where miners frequently inhale fine radioactive particles unless proper safety precautions (such as provision of masks) are taken. Miners often die of silicosis and other dust-related diseases, and the risks are increased where the dust is radioactive.

The combined costs of mining and milling uranium are, on average, about $70 per tonne of ore from an open-pit mine and about $120 per tonne from an underground mine. This kind of cost differential might make you wonder, as there is plenty of ore available, why there are any underground uranium mines operating today.

⬤ What single factor might make certain underground mines more profitable than open-pit mines?

◯ Ore grade. Remember that the costs given above are per tonne of ore — it is perfectly reasonable to mine underground if the grade of ore is high enough to offset the mining cost disadvantage.

For example, assuming, for simplicity, 100% recovery of uranium from the ore and a uranium *price* of $40 kg^{-1} (typical of the late 1980s/early 1990s), the minimum grade of ore required to break even in an operation involving an average open-pit mine works out to 1750 p.p.m. (0.175%) uranium.

Question 4

Using the same assumption, what would be the minimum 'break even' grade for an average underground mine?

The results of these calculations suggest cut-off grades higher than the figure of 350 p.p.m. which we quoted earlier, but that figure dates from a time when uranium prices were much higher. What is more, the grades we obtained are on the low side because in practice 85–90% of uranium is recovered from ores, not 100%. In addition, transportation costs of ore are not negligible, even though uranium has a *low place value* (see Block 1 *Physical Resources*, Section 2.3.1).

In fact, with the price of uranium down to about $25 kg^{-1} by 1994, most of the resources identified in Table 2 would be uneconomic.

⬤ Why is that?

◯ Cut-off grades at that price would have to be of the order of 3500 p.p.m. (0.35%) for open-pit operations, and nearly twice that for underground mines. But those would be rock-bottom break-even prices, and it would be foolish to embark on a mining venture for uranium unless the average grade were a good deal greater than those figures.

We turn now to look at the way political attitudes to nuclear power have affected the price of uranium and hence the profitability of uranium mining.

Activity 1   Uranium prices and the nuclear industry

Figure 19 gives uranium prices and production statistics for two decades that were highly influential in the development of attitudes to nuclear power. Uranium provides an excellent example of how prices and markets influence resource industries, in ways that have nothing to do with geology.

Look at Figure 19 and consider the following:

1   What was the time lag between price rises and production increases during the mid-to late 1970s and how do you explain it?

2   What was the reason for the very sharp price rise in the mid-1970s?

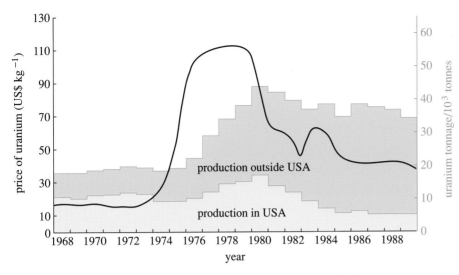

Figure 19 Uranium prices and production statistics from 1968 to 1989. Note that the left-hand axis and black curve refer to market price. The histograms for production in the USA and the rest of the world relate to the right-hand axis; for example, world production in 1980 was almost 45 000 tonnes.

3   What was the reason for the sharp *fall* in price in 1979–80, and the somewhat irregular decline thereafter (especially the 'blip' in the early 1980s)?

4   Is there any obvious evidence in Figure 19 that the Chernobyl accident in 1986 (Section 2.3.1) had a significant effect on prices or production of uranium?

5   In real terms, how do you think that uranium prices in 1968 compared with those in 1989? (Make your own estimate of an average inflation figure over the period, and use the Box on 'Doubling times').

6   What proportion of total world production of uranium did the USA supply in 1989 compared with its share in 1968?

7   In the light of calculations in Question 4 and related text, and the data in Table 2, why is it not necessarily correct to assume that more high-cost underground mines would have closed during the 1980s than low-cost surface (open pit) mines?

8   In 1990, some 320 GW of 'nuclear electricity' were being generated worldwide (Table 1). We know from Section 2.2.1 that the average nuclear fuel requirements to generate 1000 MW are about 160 tonnes uranium per year. Making the reasonable assumption that production in 1990 was the same as in 1989, how much of the 320 GW generated in 1990 by nuclear reactors was met by production of uranium in the same year? Comment on your results in the light of the additional information that by 1990 worldwide stockpiles of uranium totalled some 140 000 tonnes.

9   Finally, do you think we were correct to state at the beginning of this Activity that the events summarized in Figure 19 'have nothing to do with geology'?

Doubling times

In Block 1 we introduced a useful rule of thumb that relates annual percentage rates of increase in price or production to doubling times. It is like compound interest, leading to exponential increases and it is very simple, and worth repeating here:

$$\frac{70}{\% \text{ rate of increase}} = \text{doubling time in years}$$

So, for an annual price inflation of, say, 10%, the doubling time for prices would be 70/10 = 7 years (prices would have doubled in seven years).

Naturally, we can also work out a percentage rate of increase from a doubling time, just by rearranging the expression: 70/doubling time = % rate of increase. *Important:* The relationship breaks down for very large or very small rates.

Activity 1 was about uranium, but we could apply it to any physical resource, and the same basic economics would apply.

Figure 19 finishes at 1989, and so did Activity 1. But the nuclear industry did not close down then. Even though price and production of uranium continued their gentle downward slide into the 1990s, some 300 GW of nuclear electricity was still being generated worldwide in 1994. Put another way, to keep our industrial society supplied with the electricity it needs, something like 50 000 tonnes of uranium have to be produced *annually* (even if some of it does come from the stockpile mentioned in item 8 of Activity 1).

To produce that annual requirement of uranium, at least 10 to 20 *million* tonnes of rock waste have been produced from uranium mines, and that waste has had to be disposed of somehow. Moreover, the 50 000 tonnes of new fuel supplied to reactors each year replaces an equivalent amount of 'spent fuel', which has to be stored somewhere, whether or not it is reprocessed (see Section 2.3.2).

These numbers look terrifying when put in that way. But they are global aggregates. An individual nuclear power station will probably produce about 100 tonnes of spent fuel annually, since most are not even rated at 1000 MW, and a sustained output of 600 MW would probably be considered good. As the density of uranium is around 20 tonnes m^{-3}, the total amount of spent fuel produced at an average reactor each year has a volume of:

 … how much?

 100 tonnes of material of density 20 t m^{-3} = 100/20 = 5 m^3. That is the equivalent of a cube measuring 1.7 m (5.5 feet) on side. Put like that, it does not seem such a big storage problem, does it?

The question is whether the nuclear industry can break free from the shackles that have restricted its growth, especially now that there is a growing international desire to reduce carbon dioxide emissions. Even without expansion, however, would *reserves* and *resources* of uranium be sufficient to keep the nuclear industry going at the relatively low levels of the early 1990s (i.e. at around 300 GW total capacity)?

A good assessment of the available resources was facilitated by the boom period of the late 1970s (Figure 19). In the uranium industry, uranium *reserves* and *conditional resources* are usually referred to as **reasonably assured resources**. This includes uranium that almost certainly exists and can be mined at a price which may (reserves) or may not (conditional resources) be economic depending on the state of the market. In addition, there are *hypothetical resources* which, in the uranium industry, are known as **estimated additional resources**. These are the poorly quantified resources that may form extensions to well-explored deposits, and also include those that may just not have been evaluated because of inaccessibility and/or lack of strategic national importance. It has also become customary to quantify both kinds of resources in two production price categories: less than $80 kg^{-1} and $80–130 kg^{-1} (1990 prices), reflecting the price ranges that would apply if and when the industry next entered a boom period. Resources priced in excess of $130 kg^{-1} are excluded for the obvious reason that they would be unlikely to become economic reserves in the foreseeable future.

In the early 1990s, known uranium reserves and resources, as defined above (i.e. at less than $130 kg^{-1}), totalled some 3.5 million tonnes in countries outside the former Soviet Republics and China (whose land areas are so vast that they could contain half as much again, bringing the total to around 5 million tonnes). Eighty per cent of the total 'Western' inventory of uranium lies in just five regions: Australia, North America, southern Africa, West Africa

(specifically Niger) and South America (specifically Brazil) (see Figure 16).
Most are in areas on or near Precambrian cratons, which are often the most
fruitful areas for uranium mineralization (Section 2.2.1), and they are where
intense exploration efforts have been made to discover and produce the uranium
resources. Comparable efforts in other favourable areas could significantly
increase the total. However, that total does include uranium priced at up to
$130 kg^{-1}, which is greatly in excess of the $25 kg^{-1} or so prevailing in the mid-
1990s. Nevertheless, even if only half a million tonnes of the total reserves is
available at the lower price, a steady consumption of 50 000 tonnes per year
would give that portion of the reserves a lifetime of:

 ... how long?

 The lifetime would be 0.5×10^6 t/5×10^4 t y^{-1} = 10 years, so there is
probably plenty of uranium available to take the nuclear industry into
the twenty-first century without significant price rises.

There is the additional possibility of further supplies of enriched uranium fuel
becoming available from the dismantling of nuclear warheads in the USA and
the former Soviet Union. It has been estimated that as much as 15% of the
world's supply of nuclear fuel could be obtained this way. Even if the OECD
forecasts of 600 GW of nuclear electricity to be generated by 2030 (Section
2.1.4) were fulfilled, there would still be plenty of uranium available, because
price rises would ensure that more of the reserves and resources became
profitable, as well as encouraging further exploration. Moreover, were fast
breeder technology to become successful enough to be commercially viable on
a large scale, requirements for newly mined uranium could actually decrease.

 Why?

 Because fast breeders use mostly spent fuel from burner reactors, and
the world is awash with spent fuel.

But all this is highly speculative. The future is uncertain because every
nation that produces and/or consumes nuclear fuels needs to make balanced
judgements about the competing technical, economic and environmental
factors affecting nuclear power generation. The next and final Section on
nuclear energy discusses some of these factors.

Question 5

Figure 20 shows how categories of uranium reserves (reasonably assured
resources) changed as the price of uranium experienced its greatest rise and
fall during the 1970s.

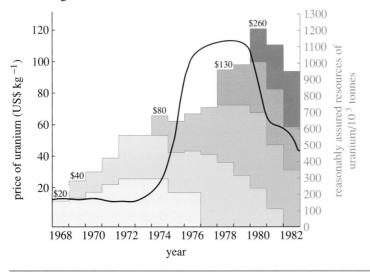

Figure 20 Historical changes in the reasonably assured resources of uranium metal in the USA by category of estimated extraction cost (dollars per kilogram) for each year from 1968 to 1982 (histograms), in relation to uranium price (line graph).

The form of stacked area diagrams such as those in Figures 19 and 20 may be unfamiliar to you, so here is how to use them. For example, in Figure 20 the reasonably assured resources at \$40 to \$80 kg^{-1} in 1978 were $(750 - 400) \times 10^3 = 350 \times 10^3$ t.

(a) To what extent would you be justified in correlating progressive darkening of the colour towards the upper right in the diagram with a progressive decrease in the grade of profitably extractable uranium ores?

(b) Do you think that the progressive disappearance of lower cost reserves of uranium with time in Figure 20 is a consequence of exhaustion of those reserves? Or is there some other explanation?

(c) Does Figure 20 provide a good illustration of how rocks can become ores (and vice versa) almost overnight, according to the whims of the market?

(d) By way of revision of basic economic concepts introduced in Block 1:

   (i) Use Figures 19 and 20 to sketch a *single* supply–price curve, and then a series of *three* demand–price curves, to represent the state of the uranium market in the late 1960s, the mid-1970s, and the late 1980s, allowing for the effects of inflation on uranium price. (A single S-curve is an over-simplification, but the exercise is easier if a fixed supply–price relationship is assumed.)

   (ii) Explain why we were able to state earlier that uranium is a commodity with low place value.

Thorium as nuclear fission fuel

The scenario you sketched in Question 5(d) could change radically if the use of nuclear energy were to expand in accordance with projections summarized in Section 2.1.4, perhaps in response to the need to reduce CO_2 emissions and/or to save fossil fuels for other uses (such as transportation or petrochemicals).

Increased demand for uranium and depletion of reserves extractable at less than \$130 kg^{-1} (1990 prices) could make an alternative fissionable fuel attractive. Thorium (Th) can be used instead of uranium, and there is much more thorium than uranium in the Earth's crust. The fission chain can be summarized as:

$$Th\text{-}232 + neutrons \rightarrow Th\text{-}233 \xrightarrow{\beta \text{ decay}} U\text{-}233$$

$$U\text{-}233 + neutrons \rightarrow fission\ products + energy\ (+ more\ neutrons)$$

Research into thorium-based nuclear reactors was already in progress in the early 1990s. Moreover, as noted earlier, if fast breeders do turn out to have a future, the reserves picture for nuclear fission fuels would change dramatically.

2.3 Side-effects of the nuclear power industry

Nuclear power generation involves concentrated fissionable fuels which, after fission, leave significant quantities of product isotopes, some of which are highly radioactive. Much of the criticism levelled against the industry falls under four main headings to which we have alluded in preceding Sections:

1 the operational safety of the reactors;

2 the biological effects of abnormal radiation levels arising from fuel transport, processing and reprocessing;

3 disposal of radioactive waste;

4 the increased potential for proliferation of nuclear weapons.

We shall not concentrate on the implications of item 4 above, noting only that there is so much uranium and plutonium easily available nowadays that those wishing to purchase materials for nuclear weapons have little difficulty in doing so. For example, the smuggling of plutonium or enriched uranium from the former Soviet Union became public knowledge in the mid-1990s. Only small amounts are required to produce the high concentrations of uranium-235 or plutonium-239 needed for a nuclear fission bomb, and it is almost impossible to guarantee effective international control over nuclear weapons — despite the existence of the UN's Non-Proliferation Treaty.

2.3.1 Reactor safety: the Chernobyl incident

By far the worst nuclear reactor accident took place on 26 April 1986 when one of four 1000 MW reactors at Chernobyl in the Ukraine released a radioactive cloud several orders of magnitude more serious than that from the Three Mile Island incident (Section 2.1.4). The build-up to this accident has been related to a series of complex chemical reactions induced by operator errors during preparation for tests on the reactor, a kind of PWR but with a graphite moderator, normally operating at 700 °C. It appears that the tests required operation at 20–25% of full power but that as the power was being reduced, an order was issued to delay the tests because of unexpected electricity demand. This series of events led to the control rods being raised, leaving in the reactor core less than the minimum number specified in the operating instructions. Once the test did proceed, the reactor was extremely difficult to control in this state and it should have shut down automatically. But again the operators intervened, retaining manual control, and as the power output fell, the reactor core started to heat up rapidly. Once it was realized that an accident was imminent, the control rods could not be replaced fast enough. The temperature and power both rose critically, leading to a massive explosion as molten uranium interacted with cooling water. The 2000-tonne reactor cap (cf. Figure 10) was lifted off, a fire started that took ten days to bring under control, and massive amounts of radioactive fission products were carried by a gas plume high into the atmosphere where they were dispersed by the wind.

The local effects of radiation were severe, with 31 fatalities and 200 incidences of radiation sickness among those working to bring the site under control. Some 130 000 people were evacuated and there were widespread restrictions on the use of fresh foods. After a week, radioactivity had spread across Western Europe (Figure 21). Parts of the UK were subjected to heavy

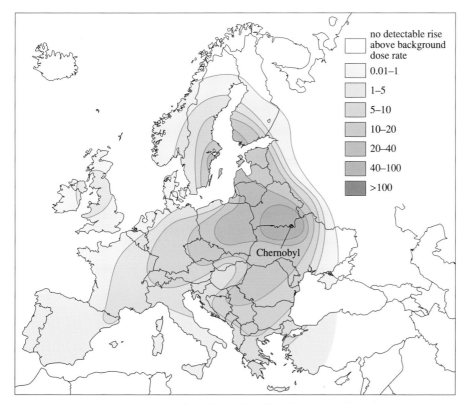

no detectable rise above background dose rate

0.01–1

1–5

5–10

10–20

20–40

40–100

>100

Chernobyl

Figure 21 The dispersion of radiation across Europe on 3 May 1986, one week after the Chernobyl accident. Note that 0.01 increase represents an increase of 1% of the (natural) background dose rate, and 1–5 represents an increase of 10–50%.

rainfall when the dispersion cloud was overhead, leading to contamination of agricultural land and moorland, particularly by radioactive caesium. Enhanced caesium levels, though below the danger threshold, were still being found in sheep in the mid-1990s in parts of north-west Britain. But the major legacy of this accident will be felt in the Russian Republics close to Chernobyl where high radiation doses have increased the risk of cancer deaths among millions of people. To be fair, the statistical probability of death by cancer has probably been raised by just a few per cent among the great majority of these people, many of whom will live for several decades. So it is unlikely that the true death toll from Chernobyl will ever be known, though estimates in the tens of thousands are not unreasonable.

Chernobyl taught us important lessons about reactor safety procedures, about the distribution of radioactivity when a reactor gets out of control, and about long-term clean-up operations which continued for several years. In particular, risk assessment studies have been improved, and in the UK, for example, where it is reasonably claimed that a Chernobyl-like accident could not occur, efforts have been redoubled to assess the risk of seismic disturbance at reactor sites. Such assessments recognize that however well we control the chance of failure due to human error, nuclear reactors can never be totally immune from natural hazards that could trigger accidents. There are over 400 reactors operating in the world today (Table 1), so these are risks that we have to live with.

An example to illustrate this point comes from the former USSR, whose nuclear industry has lagged somewhat behind that in the West. The Armenian earthquake of 1988 (which killed 25 000 people) led to closure of the 850 MW generating plant at Metsanor (near Yerevan), not because it was damaged — it was 100 km from the epicentre — but because after Chernobyl there were fears that another large earthquake could have more serious consequences. The closure led to severe power shortages in the region, but the plant was still closed in 1994.

However, natural hazards may pose less of a threat than the vagaries of human behaviour in regions less well regulated than the USA and Western Europe, where accidents can still happen (Section 2.1.4). Since the ending of the Cold War and fragmentation of the former Soviet Union, this whole vast region has become littered with dilapidated nuclear installations including power stations, waste storage and reprocessing plants, redundant missile silos, and abandoned submarine propulsion reactors — all requiring skilled maintenance that decentralized and disorganized administrations can no longer provide. In April 1993 a nuclear complex about 25 km from the Siberian city of Tomsk was damaged by an explosion and fire, a chemical accident attributed to operator error, which caused considerable contamination of the surrounding area, though not on the scale of Chernobyl. Several other nuclear plants in the former USSR were being described in 1994–95 as 'nuclear time bombs'.

In fact, there is evidence that standards of nuclear safety in the former USSR have always left something to be desired. For example, from about the mid-1960s onwards, the Soviet Navy appears to have solved its nuclear waste problems by dumping several disused submarine reactors (some with fuel still inside) in the Barents and Kara Seas (i.e. well within the Arctic Circle), along with thousands of canisters of nuclear waste.

2.3.2 Nuclear fuel transport and processing

Most radioactive materials connected with the UK nuclear power industry are transported by rail in massive transport flasks which, in tests, have been shown to survive high-speed impacts without fracturing. In fact, it is the highly radioactive spent nuclear fuels being transported to reprocessing sites that constitute the greatest danger. We shall come to this shortly. First we consider processing of the relatively innocuous yellowcake into nuclear fuel rods.

Purified uranium oxide (UO_3) is first produced from yellowcake (Figure 18) and is then either reduced in a stream of hydrogen gas to produce uranium metal with the natural 235/238 ratio, as required for Magnox reactors, or is dissolved in hot hydrogen fluoride to produce gaseous uranium hexafluoride. This can be enriched (Section 2.1.2), either in a gas centrifuge or by gaseous diffusion through a porous membrane, to increase the uranium 235/238 ratio (both processes depending on the small mass differences between atoms of uranium-235 and uranium-238), after which UO_2 is generated by heating with hydrogen and steam (Figure 22). Fuel rods (nowadays mostly of uranium oxide; Section 2.1.2; Plates 44 and 45) are then machined behind a transparent radiation shield. In general, these rather nasty chemical processes are regarded as of low risk to the workers involved; indeed, contact with hydrogen fluoride, a particularly offensive substance that rapidly dissolves human tissues, is probably a greater hazard than radiation exposure. There are, of course, waste products from this process, mostly in the form of thorium and of depleted uranium (Section 2.1.3) with a lower than normal 235/238 ratio; both have very long half-lives, so they are not strongly radioactive (see also Figure 23).

The production of *radioactive wastes* occurs chiefly as a consequence of electricity generation and fuel reprocessing. Power stations themselves unavoidably discharge gaseous radioactivity into the atmosphere, but this is sufficiently dilute not to be regarded as clinically hazardous. However, the spent fuel rods are a different problem.

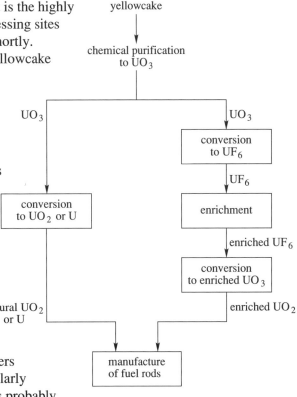

Figure 22 Stages in the chemical processing of raw uranium oxide (yellowcake) into nuclear fuel pellets.

What are the main chemical changes that occur during the active lifetime of a fuel rod in a burner reactor?

The total uranium content will decrease as fission products are generated, mainly from uranium-235 (Equation 2.2). Thus the uranium becomes depleted (Section 2.1.3) and, in addition, small amounts of plutonium are formed (Figure 7a). In fact, fuel rods are removed before all the fissile uranium has been used up because some of the accumulating fission products impede the fission reaction efficiency (as noted in Section 2.1.2).

The fission products are highly radioactive, and the result is an overall radioactivity typically about eight orders of magnitude higher than in the fresh fuel — hence the potential danger which spent fuel rods present if exposed to the environment. Many countries with a nuclear power capability simply store the spent fuel rods on site with other radioactively contaminated materials. However, several countries, notably France and the UK, have developed nuclear waste reprocessing facilities, so spent fuel must be removed and transported to the reprocessing site. At Sellafield (Cumbria), the state-owned company British Nuclear Fuels Ltd (BNFL) reprocesses depleted spent fuel to recover uranium and plutonium isotopes which can be converted into a new generation of fuel rods.

The Sellafield reprocessing facility

Formerly known as Windscale, this plant was created in the 1950s for the production of military plutonium. However, development of the Magnox reactor programme meant that Sellafield was the obvious place to reprocess spent uranium metal fuel rods, principally to retrieve plutonium for the fast breeder programme. Little of this plutonium has yet been used and, although some has been traded with the USA, stockpiles of both plutonium and radioactive waste have grown since the early 1960s.

(A little known but interesting minor use of plutonium is to provide electrical power for larger satellites and space stations. The plutonium-238 isotope has a half-life of 80 years and generates a lot of heat (see Figure 23), which is converted to electricity.)

With the advent of AGRs and PWRs on the world scene it became clear that large quantities of spent oxide fuels would be produced. In 1977, after a 100-day public enquiry, plans were approved for an extension to the site to include a new reprocessing and vitrification plant known as **THORP** (Thermal Oxide Reprocessing Plant). The object of vitrification is to concentrate the most radioactive fission products into a small volume of solid glass for disposal.

THORP was designed to cater beyond the needs of the UK nuclear programme. Its total cost, £2.8 billion over a 15-year building and development programme, was funded by contract customers paying up-front fees for reprocessing, principally the Japanese and German nuclear generating companies which, throughout the 1980s, were sending their spent fuel to Sellafield. Not surprisingly, this led to accusations that Britain was becoming a nuclear dustbin. In 1992 two critical factors further inflamed the ever-controversial status of THORP.

1   As the January 1993 start-date for the plant approached, new environmental objections were raised and the state-owned company BNFL was forced to admit that there would be an eight-fold increase of radioactive krypton-85 gas emissions from the Sellafield plant, though they believed this would pose no health risk (but they were further embarrassed early in 1993 by another accident which resulted in leakage of radioactive materials, including plutonium dust).

2   The UK Government announced the run-down of the fast-breeder research programme, thus undermining one of the principal objectives of THORP, to produce plutonium for fast breeders. In fact, there *is* an alternative use for plutonium: in MOX (Mixed OXide) fuel, in which a small proportion (10–20%) of plutonium oxide (PuO_2) is mixed with uranium oxide (UO_2), for use in PWRs. This is a means both of using up plutonium produced by reprocessing and of reducing the need to mine and process uranium ores. Its proponents estimate that by the end of the century the use of MOX could save more than 2000 tonnes of uranium annually, about 4% of the Western world's requirements (and it is being used by the nuclear industry in France). However, it would be an

exaggeration to claim that MOX is essential, given that there is plenty of cheap uranium available, and it has been estimated that the mid-1990s price of uranium (about $25 kg^{-1}$) would have to treble for MOX to be economic.

The other principal objective of THORP was to recycle uranium in the face of an anticipated shortfall in supplies.

 How reasonable was this concern at the time when THORP was first mooted in the mid-1970s?

 Eminently so, for uranium production was rising rapidly at this time (Figures 19 and 20) and continued in 1977, the time of the public inquiry.

By the early 1990s the somewhat parlous state of the nuclear industry, and the reserves and stockpiles to which we referred earlier, combined to make the reprocessing of spent fuel an uneconomic proposition. Moreover, a report from the pressure group Greenpeace, commenting that nuclear costs would be reduced by adopting long-term storage rather than a 'reprocessing and disposal' strategy, influenced Scottish Nuclear to relinquish its option on reprocessing by BNFL. Similar questions about the long-term economics of reprocessing spent fuel at THORP were raised in Germany and Japan, two of the principal customers. Japan in particular already had a significant stockpile of plutonium (about five tonnes in storage plus another five at THORP and at reprocessing facilities in France) and was planning to build its own facility. There were also strong representations from members of the US Congress that the project should be halted, on environmental grounds and because of the increased potential danger of nuclear proliferation.

The future of the expensive THORP plant looked bleak and there were questions about whether the plant should even open. The prospect was looming of the UK Treasury being forced to repay the contract customers £9 billion plus interest if the plant did not reprocess their spent fuels (instead of possibly reaping the benefits of a profit of £500 million in the first 10 years of operation). Equally serious was the prospect that a total of some 5000 jobs would be lost if the plant did not open, causing hardship and deprivation in a region where there is little alternative employment. In the event, the UK Government finally gave the green light for THORP to go ahead, in March 1994, but there remained no guarantee that it would be profitable, given the world surpluses of uranium and plutonium, and continued opposition by environmental groups. The situation was not improved by cancellation of a major German contract for fuel reprocessing in December 1994 (though this was somewhat offset by a new agreement in 1995 to process spent fuel for Scottish Nuclear). The whole story provides a classic example of how long *lead times* can result in major projects becoming less profitable (and even less socially acceptable) than was anticipated when they were begun.

As with the power stations themselves, so with nuclear fuel transport and processing, it seems that accidents present the greatest environmental risk to human populations. Table 3 puts into perspective global radioactivity emissions, illustrating that under *normal* operating conditions the nuclear industry as a whole contributes a very small fraction above *natural background radiation* (i.e. mainly incoming cosmic radiation and that emitted by natural radioactivity in rocks). The problem is that radiation leaks around nuclear facilities may be highly concentrated, making Table 3 deceptive. For example, there is evidence of above-average incidences of childhood leukaemia at Sellafield. Exposure of the children's fathers at the pre-conception stage is one suggested explanation, but this has been disputed, and other studies have found childhood leukaemias at other sites not adjacent to nuclear facilities. Another accusation levelled at Sellafield is the discharge and widespread dispersion of liquid wastes containing low levels of radioactivity into the Irish Sea through pipelines 2.5 km long. The early wastes discharged contained some particulate plutonium which, following the intervention of a Royal Commission on Environmental Protection, is now removed. Radioactive discharges are now at a minute fraction of their original levels. But this opens up the whole question of radioactive waste containment and disposal which we examine in the next Section.

Table 3 Average annual radiation exposures in the global environment, relative to average natural background (= 100)

Natural background	100
Chernobyl (1986–87 only)	1.25
weapons testing (1986, 10% of 1963)	0.4
phosphate industry*	0.25
Sellafield fire (1957 only)	0.01
nuclear industry	0.008
Three-Mile Island (1979 only)	0.0002

* Phosphates contain low natural abundances of uranium; they are widely distributed as fertilizers, giving rise to widespread low levels of radiation.

2.3.3 Radioactive waste disposal

Most fission products from nuclear reactors are solid at ordinary temperatures. They cluster around atomic mass numbers 90 and 140 (see, for example, Equation 2.2). From the point of view of waste disposal, the problem is that most of them are highly radioactive.

Among the common radioactive isotopes produced in nuclear reactors with their half-lives, are:

krypton-85 ($^{85}_{36}$Kr), 10.7 years

strontium-90 ($^{90}_{38}$Sr), 28 years

zirconium-93 ($^{93}_{40}$Zr), 1.5×10^6 years

iodine-131 ($^{131}_{53}$I), 8 days

caesium-135 ($^{135}_{55}$Cs), 2×10^6 years

caesium-137 ($^{137}_{55}$Cs), 30 years

cerium-142 ($^{142}_{58}$Ce), 5×10^5 years

Besides these fission products, there also occurs a range of heavy isotopes similar in mass and atomic number to plutonium and uranium and known as *actinide isotopes*. Together, these contribute to the waste products from nuclear reactors. Bearing in mind the quantities of each radioactive product and its half-life, we can construct an overall **decay curve** representing the gradual conversion of these materials to non-radioactive isotopes. Figure 23 is such a curve for the fission products and actinide isotopes produced in a 1 GW advanced gas-cooled reactor and expressed in terms of the heat output from radioactive decay — in other words, the heat output provides a measure of the level of radioactivity. Clearly there is a large fall in the radioactivity after about 600 years. But it is widely agreed that it is inadvisable for this waste to enter the biosphere for the next 10^3 years, and preferably the next 10^4–10^5 years. Moreover, it is vital to cool the waste in well-shielded temporary storage for the first few decades until some of the short-lived isotopes have decayed. It is important to stress that the shorter the half-life the more intense the radioactivity. So spent fuel rods (and the waste produced from them) are much more dangerous than new fuel rods, which consist of uranium with a very long half-life.

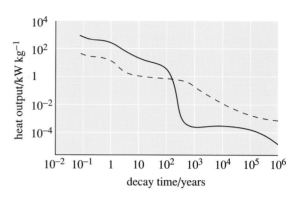

Figure 23 Change with time of the heat output from the actinides (solid line) and radioactive fission products (dashed line) from the spent fuel elements of a 1 GW advanced gas-cooled reactor.

The wastes produced by the nuclear industry, together with those from other medical and scientific practices, are subdivided for disposal purposes into those with low, intermediate and high levels of radioactivity.

Low-level wastes (LLW) include: *gases* with short half-lives, a few years at the most (mainly isotopes of hydrogen, argon, krypton, xenon and radon), which are vented to (and diluted by) the atmosphere: *liquids*, produced during waste treatment, which are discharged into the sea or rivers; and *solids* which include worn-out equipment, crushed glassware, protective clothing, air filters etc. which are burnt in incinerators and hitherto have been buried in purpose-built tips, such as Drigg in Cumbria (Figure 9). Some 40 000 m³ of low-level waste is produced annually in the UK, but its disposal is not a major environmental problem. For example, it is often pointed out that some natural substances, such as brazil nuts and coffee beans, are sufficiently radioactive to be classified as low-level wastes.

Intermediate-level wastes (ILW) have higher activities and so require more elaborate storage. They include solid and liquid materials from power stations, such as fuel cladding cans, and wastes from the radioisotope industry (e.g. hospital radiography departments) and from defence establishments. There are various sludges and resins involved and, in total, some 5000 m³ are produced annually in the UK.

High-level wastes (HLW) are the concentrated products of nuclear fuel reprocessing, containing over 95% of the total radioactivity from the nuclear industry's waste products. At present HLW is stored as low-density liquid, of which there is about 1500 m³ at Sellafield; this is contained in double-skinned stainless steel tanks surrounded by concrete and cooled by sets of stainless-steel coils through which water is circulated (Plate 46). It is this waste that may ultimately be solidified into borosilicate glass (see Box on 'THORP'), which could then be incorporated into a thermodynamically stable multiple containment system (Figure 24) ready for disposal.

In volume terms, HLW are not a large problem; Figure 7 shows that 4800 tonnes of new fuel end up as 4650 t of spent fuel after 30 years, and 4800 − 4650 = 150 t of fission products. It is that which becomes HLW after

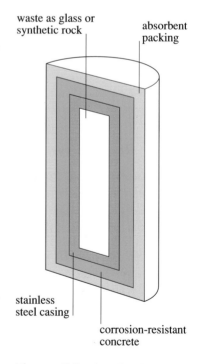

Figure 24 A cylindrical multiple containment system suitable for burial of high-level nuclear waste in a deep borehole and resistant over a long period (100–1000 years) to the effects of groundwater penetration.

reprocessing. At an average density of $10\,t\,m^{-3}$, the total volume of HLW produced by a 1 GW burner reactor after 30 years is $150\,t/10\,t\,m^{-3} = 15\,m^3$, the space occupied by a few large wardrobes.

Even though these fission products remain extremely radioactive for centuries (Figure 23), the storage and disposal problem for HLW seems relatively small in volume terms, compared with the question of where spent fuel is to be stored, whether reprocessed or not. After 30 years the volume of spent fuel is ten times greater than the volume of HLW produced: about $150\,m^3$ (compare the calculation on page 32) — but even that needs a space no bigger than a medium-sized swimming pool.

The job of developing and implementing a policy for dealing with solid LLW and ILW has been given to UK NIREX (the Nuclear Industry Radioactive Waste Executive), a company jointly owned by the different members of the UK nuclear industry. NIREX has developed a policy, to the Government's satisfaction, that early disposal should take place in a deep facility where radioactivity will be 'permanently' isolated from the environment. Responsibility for continued storage of high-level solid wastes and other liquid wastes remains with BNFL pending further research into LLW/ILW disposal sites.

Clearly, then, there is no shortage of suitable rocks in the UK, but initial proposals based on geological criteria led to immediate environmental opposition as we shall now see.

The story of UK radioactive waste disposal goes back to the 1970s when exploratory drilling was proposed in crystalline rocks (mainly granitic) in Scotland, Cornwall, mid-Wales and Northumberland. At this stage the initiative was directed towards vitrified HLW disposal. However, opposition in the form of local pressure groups backed by expert witnesses was so well organized that only in the Caithness area, at Altnabreac near Dounreay (Figure 9), was permission to drill granted. The Government abandoned its

---

Geological criteria for radioactive waste disposal

In the best of circumstances, a containment system such as the one shown in Figure 24 will last for only 100–1000 years, though the glass itself may inhibit the migration of radioactive isotopes for a further 1000 years. So, in view of the long decay times (Figure 23), the ideal geological site for disposal should also act as a barrier. On land, the prime geological contenders for waste containment in the UK are clay-rich rocks, salt deposits, and hard crystalline igneous or metamorphic rocks.

● What properties do all these rock types have in common that will be useful in impeding the migration of radioactive isotopes from nuclear wastes — not just HLW, but ILW and LLW too?

○ They are all relatively impermeable to fluid migration, and have large-scale homogeneity

and a massive structure. Salt and some clay deposits have the advantage of being self-sealing, owing to their high plasticity; clays have a high capacity for ion adsorption (i.e. ions adhere to their surfaces because ions carry an electrical charge), and crystalline rocks are generally dry, stable against geological movement, extensive and inert to any heating effect from waste canisters.

Question 6

Taking these three groups of rocks in turn (clay-rich sedimentary rocks, salt deposits and crystalline rocks), suggest (with the help of the *Postcard Geological Map*) which might be the best areas for radioactive waste disposal to be located in the UK.

HLW borehole programme in 1981 in favour of current arrangements (storage of HLW at Sellafield, see below).

In 1983 the newly formed NIREX announced that two sites for ILW/LLW disposal should be considered for detailed investigation: (a) a disused deep anhydrite mine owned by ICI at Billingham, and (b) a wartime munitions store in shallow Mesozoic clays at Elstow (near Bedford; see Figure 9). The fact that there was little prior public consultation again led to massive local objections and by 1985 the Environment Department announced that (a) Billingham was dropped and (b) NIREX should select further sites in addition to Elstow.

In 1986 three further sites were identified as possible shallow disposal repositories: a CEGB site on thick boulder clay in the port area of South Killingholme; a Ministry of Defence airfield on Mesozoic clays at Fulbeck (Figure 9); and a site on London Clay at Bradwell, next to a Magnox station in Essex. After earlier experience, the opposition to all four sites was extremely well orchestrated, and after the Chernobyl accident the Government decided to withdraw its proposal to bury ILW in shallow sites. This left LLW, but when contractors' drill rigs reached the four sites later in 1986 they were effectively blockaded by local opposition groups (would the opposition have been so well organized and enthusiastic, had the waste consisted of mouldy brazil nuts or coffee beans or other natural products with radiation levels similar to those of LLW?) A technically informed coalition of County Councils recommended that both ILW and LLW should be buried in *deep* disposal sites, and in May 1987 (with an election imminent) the Government concurred.

By 1989, proposals for a deep ILW/LLW disposal site had retreated to areas where there was already a sympathy for nuclear activity: at Sellafield and Dounreay (the so-called 'nuclear oases'). Since well over half the waste that will enter the repository will be generated at Sellafield, and since new rail links would have to be built at Dounreay, it is hardly surprising that in 1991 Sellafield became the chosen site on logistic and financial grounds. The plan is to create a network of caverns at about 500–700 m depth in crystalline rocks of the Borrowdale Volcanic Series (of Ordovician age, about 450 Ma), that will take 10^6 m³ of LLW and 3×10^5 m³ of ILW by the year 2030. Although NIREX hoped to start the 10-year construction during the late-1990s, in early 1995 they were still finding it difficult to obtain planning permission.

Oklo revisited

The 'natural reactor' at Oklo (Gabon), described in Section 2.1.2, is also a natural HLW disposal site of great antiquity (1800 Ma). It has provided a unique opportunity to study the migration of the fission products and actinides over extremely long timescales, and at a site that has not been carefully chosen to have low water flows. Not surprisingly, most of the gases (for example, krypton and xenon) have been lost. However, although alkali metals such as caesium have migrated substantial distances, only a small fraction of the lanthanide elements, such as lanthanum and samarium, have moved, and then not more than a metre from their production site. The least mobile group of radioisotopes were the actinides, including plutonium, for which migration was estimated to be of the order of *millimetres* or less. Overall, only a few per cent of the fission products migrated from the source of the nuclear reaction, a matter of several metres, in 1.8×10^9 years. The Oklo phenomenon only gives migration data relevant to that site. Nevertheless, it provides evidence that, under some circumstances, high-level waste does not migrate significantly over timescales far greater than those of interest for the disposal of radioactive waste resulting from human activities. It certainly provides a test bed for models of radioisotope transport.

NIREX spent £20 million surveying the two sites, including the drilling of deep boreholes, and geological and hydrological uncertainties about the suitability of Sellafield have become apparent. The geological structure is quite simple (Figure 25): Permo-Triassic sandstones covering the Borrowdale Volcanics dip to the west towards the Irish Sea. At first it was thought that the water-flow regimes in these two formations would be completely separate, with the volcanics being relatively impermeable. Drilling revealed, however, that the volcanics were sufficiently fractured to transmit groundwater. So, not only does circulation of fresh groundwater occur in *both* formations, the *saline intrusion* extending inland from the coast also penetrates the Borrowdale Volcanics, effectively blocking the seaward flow of groundwater, including that from around the proposed repository. Propelled by the *hydraulic head* of water in the adjacent Lake District mountains, the fresh groundwater will 'float' on top of the denser saline waters, thus migrating towards the surface on a much shorter path than anticipated. Further research efforts were directed to the resolution of this problem.

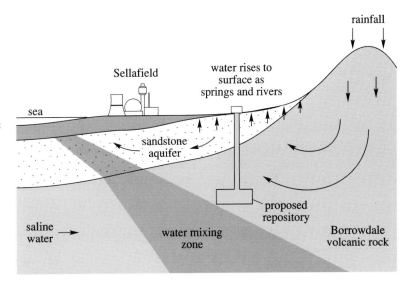

Figure 25 Cross-section through the Sellafield site to illustrate possible movement of groundwater around the proposed nuclear waste repository.

HLW produced by reprocessing will need to be stored on site at Sellafield for a long time, because the nuclear industry is not planning to dispose of HLW until at least 2080. Meanwhile the problem of waste disposal is just as acute in many other countries, several of which have technically aware environmental pressure groups. The UK nuclear industry illustrates well how such groups can successfully stimulate debate and even modify government policy. We leave you to decide whether their opposition is justified and, indeed, whether nuclear fuels should even be reprocessed at all.

2.4 Summary of Section 2

1   Nuclear power generation in reactors results from the accelerated fission of heavy uranium isotopes when bombarded by neutrons. Conventional burner reactors such as Magnox, AGRs and PWRs require the relatively scarce uranium-235 isotope, whereas fast breeder reactors (which have still not been developed on any significant scale) would exploit the more abundant uranium-238. Magnox reactors use uranium metal fuel rods with the natural 235/238 ratio, whereas AGRs and PWRs use uranium oxide fuels enriched in the 235 isotope.

2   In the early 1990s there were over 400 electricity generating nuclear reactors in operation around the world producing 16% of global electricity demand. The main producers are the USA, France, the former Soviet Republics, Japan and Germany.

3   The UK played a leading role in nuclear power developments with its 1950s Magnox programme. During the 1970s, new more efficient reactor designs led to the proliferation of AGRs in the UK, and PWRs and other analogous reactors overseas. Progress was slowed in the late 1970s as concern grew over the operational safety of nuclear reactors. Of the ten British PWRs planned in the 1980s only one (Sizewell B) survived the planning enquiries.

4   Even excluding the costs of decommissioning reactors and managing radioactive waste, nuclear power in the UK is probably more expensive than power from fossil fuels. Nevertheless, arguments that nuclear power generation produces virtually no carbon and sulphur gases, combined with technological improvements, weigh in favour of its further development.

5   The principal geochemical characteristics that determine the distribution and concentration of uranium to form ore deposits are: (a) the large charge and size of uranium ions, which makes uranium an incompatible element that is concentrated by fractional crystallization and partial melting, and so is most abundant in granitic rocks; (b) the much greater solubility of U^{6+} than of U^{4+} in surface environments, which promotes uranium transport in oxidizing groundwaters and deposition from reducing groundwaters.

6   Uranium deposits formed by internal processes (e.g. disseminated magmatic and hydrothermal vein deposits) are termed 'primary'; those formed by surface processes (e.g. sandstone-hosted and quartz-pebble conglomerate deposits) are termed 'secondary'.

7   The relatively high costs of underground compared with open-pit mining for uranium can be offset by differences in ore grade. However, the 1980s slump in uranium prices, consequent on the lower-than-anticipated growth in nuclear power demand, led to many deposits becoming uneconomic and to a stockpiled surplus of uranium.

8   Current estimates of reasonably assured and estimated additional uranium resources at less than $130 kg^{-1}$ total about 3.5 million tonnes. Even if an OECD model predicting expansion of world nuclear power generation to 600 GW by the year 2030 was to happen, the fuel required could be supplied from these reserves alone.

9   Public concerns about nuclear reactor safety were exacerbated in 1986 when automated safety procedures at the Chernobyl reactor were overridden during tests, leading to a massive explosion and the widespread atmospheric dispersion of radioactive contamination over most of Europe. The probability of death due to cancers was increased for millions of people.

10   The intensity of radiation is greater from radioactive isotopes with short half-lives (fission products) than from those with long half-lives (uranium and plutonium). The processing and reprocessing of nuclear fuels, and particularly of spent fuel rods, therefore constitute a potential hazard to those living nearby, though as at 1995 this has been tentatively linked only to increased incidences of childhood leukaemia. The small, but finite risk of accidents at facilities such as the controversial THORP plant on the Sellafield site could be much more serious.

11   Plans to dispose of radioactive waste by burial in the UK have had a chequered history, and plans to bury high-level wastes (HLW) have been postponed indefinitely. A succession of NIREX proposals for the burial of intermediate and low-level wastes (ILW and LLW) met with stubborn and well-informed local opposition leading, ultimately, to a retreat in favour of 'nuclear oases'. The economically favoured solution, a deep repository at Sellafield, suffers from questionable hydrological conditions.

12   The problem of radioactive waste disposal is equally acute in several other countries where spent fuel rods are accumulating rapidly.

Question 7

(a) In burner reactors, a moderator is used to slow down the neutrons and the position of the control rods is continually adjusted to absorb excess neutrons. Why it is necessary (i) to slow down neutrons and (ii) to absorb the excess?

(b) Figure 6 shows that there is no moderator in a fast breeder reactor. Why is this?

(c) All uranium-based reactors breed plutonium but some do so faster than others: Why is this?

(d) Why does the uranium in ore deposits not all disappear by spontaneous fission?

Question 8

Decide, giving reasons, whether each of the following statements about uranium ore deposits and their formation is true or false.

A   The charge and size of uranium ions are such that uranium does not fit readily into the crystal structures of common rock-forming minerals.

B   Mineralized fault zones, particularly those beneath erosional unconformities, provide some of the world's richest uranium deposits.

C   Uranium deposits in near-surface sandstones require higher cut-off grades to mine economically than underground vein-type ores because the former are more expensive to mine than the latter.

D   Roll-type uranium ores in sandstones form at an oxidation–reduction boundary where U^{6+} carried in groundwaters is precipitated on conversion into U^{4+}.

E   Yellowcake is an ammonium uranyl salt produced after ion-exchange treatment to purify the leachates of uranium ores.

F   Uranium minerals may be precipitated from surface waters in the anaerobic reducing environments of lagoons and coastal swamps.

Question 9

(a) Why are spent fuel rods from nuclear reactors potentially so much more serious a hazard than new fuel rods if exposed accidentally to the environment?

(b) What factors have caused the economics of nuclear fuel reprocessing in the UK to change since 1986?

(c) What is the purpose of plans to vitrify high-level radioactive wastes?

(d) Depleted uranium (Section 2.1.3) is one of the hardest and heaviest metals known and is ideal for use in tank armour and high-density warheads of missiles. In 1993 some Gulf War veterans claimed that they might have become ill through proximity to armour plating and warheads made of depleted uranium. Why do Figure 23 and related text suggest these fears could be exaggerated?

Video Band 13: *Renewable Energies*, is associated with this Block. It covers material in Sections 3 and 4, and features some of the examples cited in the text. It is scheduled for viewing after Section 4, with questions provided to reinforce your study of the text. However, if you have time you may wish to watch it before starting on the next two Sections.

3 GEOTHERMAL ENERGY

In this Section we deal with techniques of energy production that depend entirely on heat produced *within* the Earth, as outlined in the first Chapter of Block 4 *Energy 1*. The total amount of heat flowing through the Earth's surface is about 3×10^{20} J y^{-1}, generated mainly by the decay of long-lived radioactive isotopes of uranium, thorium and potassium (see Section 2.1.1). In that sense, like uranium resources for the nuclear power industry, we are dealing with another primary, internal source of energy.

As you might have inferred from Section 2.2.1, the picture that the term 'geothermal energy' often brings to mind is one of boiling mud pools, geysers and vents in volcanic areas gushing with hot steam. Traditionally, most attempts to exploit geothermal energy have relied on the drilling of boreholes in such areas to tap high-pressure steam from aquifers containing very hot water. The steam is used to drive turbines that generate electricity, in exactly the same way that steam raised by fossil fuel combustion is used in conventional power stations (Figure 2). Alternatively, the steam may be piped throughout the surrounding area for direct use in space heating and industrial processes. There are also various techniques for exploiting geothermal energy in areas with less obvious geothermal resources. One technique is to pump warm water from well-insulated deep aquifers, again for domestic and industrial heating; another seeks to produce steam for electricity generation by drilling more deeply than usual to encounter suitable hot rocks.

Throughout this Section on geothermal energy, you should bear in mind that we are dealing essentially with groundwater which just happens to be hotter than usual, and which moves through rocks in the same way as any other groundwater.

The flow of internally generated heat across the Earth's surface is fairly constant over most of the globe, ranging from 40 to 120 mW m^{-2} and averaging about 60 mW m^{-2} (milliwatts per square metre). But in certain places, where there is a close association between hot springs and volcanoes, the flow of heat may be much greater, up to 300 mW m^{-2}.

● Where, in terms of their distribution with respect to tectonic plates, are such thermally anomalous regions likely to be concentrated?

○ Most of the world's volcanoes occur at the boundaries of the tectonic plates, either at *constructive plate margins*, where new ocean lithosphere is formed as basaltic magma rises to the surface (e.g. in Iceland), or at *destructive plate margins*, where ocean lithosphere plunges back into the mantle, which undergoes partial melting to produce magmas which rise to the surface (e.g. volcanoes and geothermal centres in the Western Americas and New Zealand).

Such areas are termed **hyperthermal areas**, where water at temperatures well above 100 °C can be brought to the surface as steam for electricity generation (see Section 3.1). They have been the prime targets for past geothermal developments (Figure 26). In addition there are many **semi-thermal areas**, where hot groundwater below the boiling temperature can be exploited. But by far the greatest part of the Earth's crust is 'non-thermal' as a geothermal resource, with heat flow near or even below the global average.

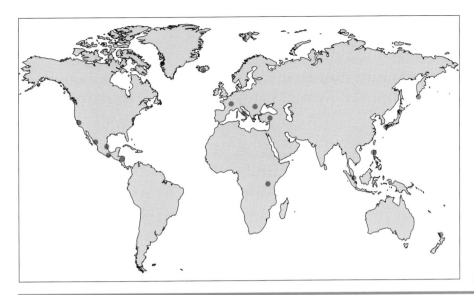

Figure 26 The main areas of geothermal energy production operating today.

The heat conductivity equation

To understand the origin of the different kinds of geothermal resource we need to know the following equation for conductive heat flow:

$$q = \frac{k\Delta T}{z} \qquad (3.1)$$

where the *heat flow* (q) is measured in W m^{-2} (watts per square metre); the *thermal conductivity* (k) is measured in W m^{-1} K^{-1} (watts per metre per (degree) Kelvin); and the temperature difference (ΔT), measured over depth (z), comprises the **geothermal gradient** (this term was introduced in Block 4 *Energy 1*, in the context of petroleum generation; it normally has units of K km^{-1}). Note that the SI temperature unit, the Kelvin, is used by convention rather than degrees Celsius, and it carries no degree symbol. The concept of thermal conductivity requires further comment. It is a measure of the ease with which a material transmits heat. Thus a metal pan has a high thermal conductivity whereas a pair of insulating gloves has a low one. All rocks are poor conductors of heat in the everyday sense, but certain rocks, such as sandstones and granites, are better conductors of heat than others, such as shales and many metamorphic rocks, which are the best insulators.

⬤ If heat flow q in Equation 3.1 is constant, will the geothermal gradient ($\Delta T/z$) be greater where the thermal conductivity (k) is high (good conductor) or where it is low (poor conductor)? In other words, for a given heat flow, will temperature increase more rapidly with depth where thermal conductivity is high or where it is low?

○ If q is constant, a lower value of k must be associated with a higher value of $\Delta T/z$ and *vice versa*. Since the question asks for a rapid increase of temperature (T) with depth (z), a *low* thermal conductivity is required.

For example, if heat flow (q) is 100 mW m^{-2}, which is 100×10^{-3} J s^{-1} m^{-2}, and if the geothermal gradient is 100 K km^{-1}, as it could be in some volcanically active areas, then from Equation 3.1:

$$100 \times 10^{-3} \text{ W m}^{-2} = \frac{100 \text{ K}}{1000 \text{ m}} \times k$$

then $$k = \frac{100 \times 10^{-3} \text{ W m}^{-2} \times 10^3 \text{ m}}{100 \text{ K}}$$

$$= 1 \text{ W m}^{-1} \text{ K}^{-1}$$

If the geothermal gradient is *less*, say 50 K km^{-1}, then for the same heat flow the thermal conductivity would need to be:

$$k = \frac{100 \times 10^{-3} \text{ W m}^{-2} \times 10^3 \text{ m}}{50 \text{ K}}$$

$$= 2 \text{ W m}^{-1} \text{ K}^{-1}$$

i.e. twice as great.

Question 10

A favourable site for geothermal development will have an above-average temperature at shallow depth, within the top few kilometres of the crust (i.e. there will be an above-average, or steeper, geothermal gradient). Leaving aside hyperthermal volcanic areas, answer the following.

(a) What rock types might produce an above-average geothermal gradient by virtue of their low thermal conductivity?

(b) What common rock types tend to be rich in uranium and so might have the same effect by virtue of their locally high radioactive heat production?

We now have the key to understanding the three main categories in geothermal energy exploitation which are considered below. In chronological order of their development these are: (a) hyperthermal volcanic zones, (b) semi-thermal zones beneath shallow, low conductivity strata, (c) semi-thermal zones characterized by rocks with high heat production. Resources of category (b) usually include aquifers containing warm water within the low conductivity strata, and this water is exploited by pumping. Those of category (c) are usually dry and must be fractured to allow heat to be extracted by pumping water from the surface down through the rocks and back up to the surface.

3.1 Resources in high-pressure steam fields

Most areas containing recently active volcanoes and/or igneous intrusions will have above-average heat flow and geothermal gradients simply because hot magmas have risen high into the crust and are still cooling. If such a hyperthermal area contains rock sequences which are permeable to groundwater circulation, then the heat will promote *fluid convection* within these sequences, as outlined in Section 2.2.1. Where the groundwater is freely able to migrate upwards, hot springs, boiling mud pools and geysers may be produced. Since volcanic activity in a given region usually lasts for a few million years and intruded magmas take a long time to cool, hyperthermal areas effectively provide a *renewable* energy resource because the water supply is usually also renewable.

⬤ By analogy with oil and gas traps, what geological conditions will be needed to prevent the upwards loss of hot geothermal fluids?

⦿ To prevent low density fluids (whether oil or gas or water) from escaping at the surface, they must be trapped beneath impermeable cover rocks. So, if geothermal resources are to be used for power production, then, as well as a heat source, permeable aquifers overlain by impermeable seals are essential.

Typically, geothermal water may be under pressures of several tons of atmospheres and at temperatures of 200 °C or more when trapped: the pressure ensures that much of the fluid is in the liquid state. For exploitation of this geothermal resource, a borehole is drilled into the reservoir which enables the fluid to be brought to the surface. At this stage, pressure is rapidly reduced, causing the fluid spontaneously to separate, or **steam flash**, into steam and liquid water. The high-temperature steam is then used to drive a turbine, generating electricity. Water extracted during production, and from hot springs and geysers, is replenished naturally by water re-entering the aquifer from a *recharge* area (see also Section 2.2.1). Increasingly, however, the spent geothermal fluid is reinjected into the aquifer through a second borehole. This is necessary to maintain fluid pressures in the aquifer and it also provides a means of reducing atmospheric pollution from gases other than water vapour (see later).

Examples of steam fields

Figure 27 is a cross-section through the Wairakei geothermal field in New Zealand, which shows how heated water travels upwards, confined at pressure within permeable layers. Faults in the area act as safety valves for the system: the steam and hot water which escape along these outlets are responsible for the surface hot springs and geysers. The aquifer at Wairakei originally contained only liquid water at high pressure, a type of geothermal field known as *water dominated*. However, as pressures have fallen during exploitation since the 1950s, a mixed steam and water zone (known as a two-phase zone) has developed above the remaining deeper liquid zone. The steam produced at the surface tends to be 'wet' (i.e. it contains condensed water droplets), and so must be 'dried' by passing through a steam–water separator to remove any liquid water before it enters the turbines.

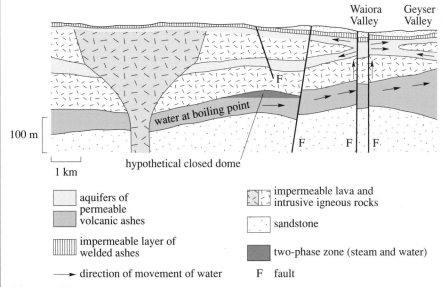

aquifers of permeable volcanic ashes

impermeable layer of welded ashes

→ direction of movement of water

impermeable lava and intrusive igneous rocks

sandstone

two-phase zone (steam and water)

F fault

Figure 27 Cross-section of the Wairakei geothermal field in New Zealand, showing deep aquifers carrying high-pressure water close to boiling point, towards the Waiora Valley. Here faults provide a channel by which the fluid may reach the surface as super-heated steam above the atmospheric boiling temperature. Note the presence of a two-phase zone in a dome where upwards circulating water is converted into steam due to a lowering of pressure. The heat source in this case is the cooling intrusive igneous body at the left.

In contrast, the geothermal field at Larderello in northern Italy, one of the world's largest and longest established areas of geothermal power production, is *steam dominated* or 'dry'. The reason the steam is free from liquid water is because the reservoir temperature is higher and the pressure lower than at Wairakei, so a dry steam zone overlies a liquid zone (analogous to gas overlying oil in a petroleum trap). The Larderello area has been producing electrical power since 1904 from steam circulating within a permeable fractured limestone which is overlain by impermeable shales and clays (Figure 28). The main source of heat is believed to be a magma body and/or a series of igneous intrusions, several kilometres below the surface. As the intrusions rose through the crust, the area became gently domed and faulted to provide a rather complex *anticlinal trap* for the hot geothermal fluids. The resources of the world's largest geothermally exploited area, the Geysers field of northern California, are very similar: dry steam is produced from fractured sandstones at 1–2 km depth beneath an impermeable cover in an area lying on the edge of a currently active volcanic arc.

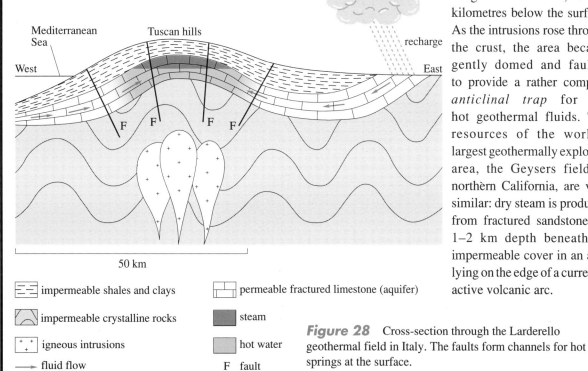

impermeable shales and clays

impermeable crystalline rocks

igneous intrusions

→ fluid flow

permeable fractured limestone (aquifer)

steam

hot water

F fault

Figure 28 Cross-section through the Larderello geothermal field in Italy. The faults form channels for hot springs at the surface.

Although the principles of generating electricity in hyperthermal steam fields are simple enough, there are considerable technical problems in drilling down to tap steam and hot water at pressures up to 30–35 atmospheres (atm) and temperatures up to 400 °C. Even at the more typical 4–5 atm and 240 °C of steam-dominated reservoirs, high-pressure steam emerges from wells with velocities of around 1000 km per hour (up to 300 m s⁻¹) and sounds like a jet engine at full throttle. This energy has to be transmitted to generator turbines with minimum loss; the transmission pipes are therefore well lagged to stop the steam condensing to form water droplets and to keep it 'dry'. During the early stages of development, steam from a well is usually passed through a turbine and vented directly to the atmosphere (often via a gas extraction unit which removes pollutants such as carbon dioxide, hydrogen sulphide and methane). Such power stations, which vent steam at just over 1 atm pressure, are known as *back-pressure power plants* (Figure 29a) because they rely entirely on the excess pressure of the geothermal steam, above 1 atm, for power production.

Figure 29 (a) A back-pressure geothermal power plant. (b) A condensation geothermal power plant in which steam on the low-pressure side of the generating turbine is condensed to increase the pressure difference across the turbine. (c) A double flash power plant. (d) A binary cycle power plant. Note that (c) and (d) are increasingly used for lower temperature geothermal resources on the fringes of hyperthermal areas.

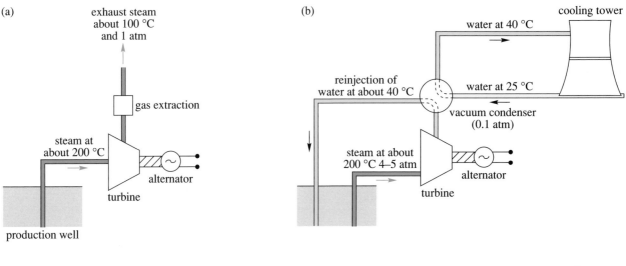

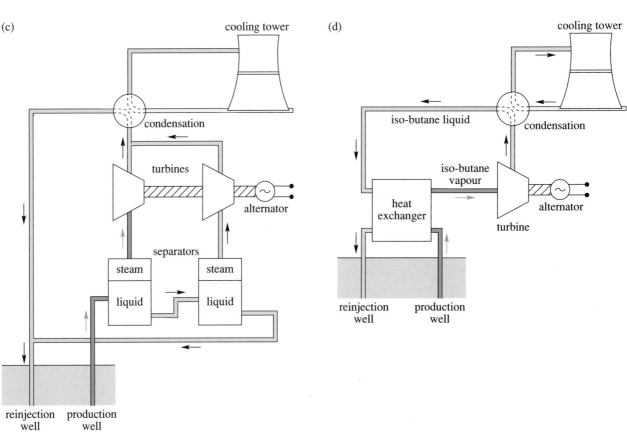

Once the output of a geothermal well has stabilized, it becomes possible to increase the efficiency of the turbine by attaching a condensation unit to the low-pressure side.

 How will condensing the steam to water help to increase the power station efficiency?

 Partly because water occupies a much smaller volume, and condensation increases the pressure drop across the turbine by a further 1 atm, and partly because condensation increases the temperature drop across the turbine, thereby improving energy conversion efficiency (see Box in Section 2.1).

Power stations of this type require cooling towers (Figure 29b) and are known as *condensation power plants*. A typical turbine produces up to 55 MW of electrical power and there might be up to four turbines in a power station. In common with most vapour power cycles, efficiencies are low; despite the use of high-temperature superheated steam they rarely exceed 30% (i.e. less than 30% of the energy contained in high-pressure hot steam is converted to electrical power).

It takes somewhere between 5 kg and 10 kg of steam to generate 1 kWh (1 kilowatt hour or 3.6×10^3 J) from hyperthermal steam fields, of both the water-dominated and steam-dominated varieties. In contrast, in the broader areas fringing these fields, large volumes of water occur at somewhat lower pressures and temperatures which are equally amenable to power generation, albeit at levels approaching 100 kg of steam per kWh. Two relatively recent power station technologies used to exploit these vast reserves have been developed, particularly for use in the western USA outside the Geysers area. They are:

1 *Double flash plant* (Figure 29c), also called *dual flash plant*. Unflashed liquid remaining after the initial, high-pressure flashing flows to a low-pressure tank where another pressure drop leads to a second flashing phase and provides additional steam. This steam is mixed with the exhaust from the high-pressure turbine to drive a second stage turbine, so raising power output by 20–25% for only a 5% increase in plant cost. Dual flash systems can also be incorporated into condensation power plants to increase their efficiency further.

2 *Binary cycle plant* (Figure 29d). This type of power plant uses a secondary working fluid with a lower boiling point than water, such as pentane or butane, which is vaporized and used to drive the turbine. The obvious advantage is that low temperature resources can be exploited where single or dual flash systems have proved unsatisfactory. The geothermal water is pumped at reservoir pressure through a heat exchange unit, a kind of double radiator system, and is then reinjected. The thermal energy supplied, ideally, is adequate to superheat the secondary fluid. Although higher efficiencies have been produced than in steam flash plants, and many units of this type are in operation, the capital costs are inevitably high.

Despite these complications, electrical power is being produced at competitive costs from many hyperthermal areas; for example, the cost per kWh of electricity from the Geysers field fell from 8.5 cents in 1981 to 5.7 cents in 1992. Table 4 shows that some 5.8 GW of geothermal electrical power was being produced in the early 1990s. It accounts for 1.5% of Italy's electricity requirements, 10% of New Zealand's, and is becoming important in many other volcanically active circum-Pacific countries. Just how rapid is the growth rate, and how influential are hyperthermal resources on the world energy scene?

Table 4   World geothermal resources exploited in the early 1990s

	Electrical (MW$_{electrical}$)	Non-electrical (MW$_{equivalent}$)
Americas		
USA	2800	160
Mexico	680	8
El Salvador	95	–
Nicaragua	35	–
Western Pacific		
Japan	228	970
China	11	610
Taiwan	3	10
Philippines	894	–
Indonesia	140	–
New Zealand	280	200
Europe, Asia, Africa		
Former Soviet Republics	11	340
Iceland	39	480
France	4	270
Italy	545	210
Hungary	–	375
Turkey	21	70
Azores	3	–
Kenya	45	–
others	–	420
totals	5834	4123

Question 11

(a) World geothermal electricity capacity was 720 MW in 1969, and 2900 MW in 1981. If the value of 5834 MW in Table 4 represents the picture in 1992, what were the approximate historic growth rates in the two periods 1969–81 and 1981–92? Assume growth was exponential and make use of the Box in Section 2.2.2. Determine the doubling time for each of the two periods first.

(b) World-wide total energy demand was about 3.4×10^{20} J in 1992. What was the percentage contribution from all geothermal sources to this total? (1 MW = 3.15×10^{13} J y^{-1})

A contribution of less than a tenth of one per cent to global energy demand may seem like a negligible 'drop in the ocean', but in Question 11(b) we are considering contributions to *total* energy rather than to *electrical* energy production. In fact, geothermal power has steadily increased its share of the electricity market and represented about 0.3% of the world's electrical needs in the early 1990s. The proportion is increasing, and there is potential for growth to a few per cent in the coming decades.

Table 4 also includes contributions from semi-thermal areas where hot water can be produced, as we shall see in Section 3.2. These appear in the 'non-electrical' column, along with contributions from steam and hot water in hyperthermal regions used for district heating schemes, horticulture, aquaculture and even for domestic hot water systems. For example, well over half the population of Iceland gets its domestic hot water from geothermal sources, and the original steam fields in Reykjavik are still producing at undiminished capacity after 50 years. The cost to the Icelandic consumer of piped geothermal heating is only 25–30% of what it would cost for equivalent oil-fired heating. The *total* contribution of about 4 GW (Table 4) of equivalent geothermal power for non-electrical uses is substantial and in several countries it far exceeds the amount supplied as electricity.

Environmental impact of geothermal steam fields

Geothermal 'pollutants' are chiefly confined to the non-condensable gases, mainly carbon dioxide (CO_2) with lesser amounts of hydrogen sulphide (H_2S) or sulphur dioxide (SO_2), hydrogen (H_2), methane (CH_4) and nitrogen (N_2). In the condensed water there is also dissolved silica, along with calcium, sodium and potassium chlorides in variable quantities. These can be precipitated as pressure falls and cause scaling and blockage in the pipes, but techniques have been developed to prevent this and the dissolved salts are nowadays reinjected, which also removes the problem of dealing with waste water. Traditionally, geothermal sites have received a bad press on account of their association with the rotten eggs smell of hydrogen sulphide (H_2S). However, this and other gaseous products of old leaking plant have now been minimized so that the environmental impact of geothermal production is at a minimum. Interestingly, the level of atmospheric H_2S in the air over the Geysers field is now lower than was produced from hot springs and geysers before geothermal developments began; this has been achieved mainly by gas extraction, involving the production of huge quantities of unwanted sulphur, rather than by reinjection, which was recently introduced in California.

The facts are now quite plain — geothermal developments have a net *positive* impact on the environment compared with conventional energy systems, because of their much smaller pollution effects. Watt for watt, modern geothermal plants emit less than 0.2% of the greenhouse gas CO_2 than does the cleanest fossil fuel plant (Figure 30). Comparable figures for the acid rain gas SO_2 and for particulates are less than 1% and 0.1% respectively. In terms of social developments, geothermal plant requires very little land, taking up no more than a hectare or two for plant sizes of 100 MW or more. Geothermal drilling, with no risk of fire, is safer than oil or gas drilling, and although there have been a few steam blowout events, there is far less potential for environmental damage from drilling accidents. In direct-use applications, geothermal units are operated in a closed cycle, mainly to minimize corrosion and scaling problems, and there are no emissions. So while the acidic saline

fluids are corrosive to machinery, such as pumps and turbines, these represent technological challenges rather than environmental hazards.

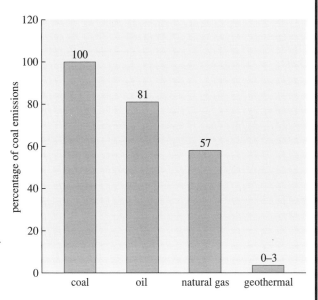

Figure 30 Comparative CO_2 emissions for fossil fuel and geothermal power plants. (100% is equivalent to 7700 tonnes of carbon as CO_2 per megawatt year.)

Geothermals and hydrothermals

The heated groundwaters that we have been discussing here as an energy source are also hydrothermal solutions. They dissolve elements from the rocks through which they pass, because they are 'acidic saline fluids' (and therefore corrosive), commonly containing several grams per litre of dissolved salts (especially chlorides of sodium, potassium, calcium) and up to several hundred p.p.m. of dissolved metals (copper, lead, zinc, silver and even uranium). It is these dissolved constituents that cause the problems of scaling in pipes, because the pipes provide environments analogous to fissures and cracks in rocks where hydrothermal solutions cool and deposit minerals to form ores. In short, present-day geothermal fields are also active hydrothermal systems and provide much information about how hydrothermal ore deposits (not only of uranium, Section 2.2.1, but of other metals too) have formed. Many hydrothermal ore provinces are simply fossil geothermal fields.

3.2 Resources from shallow, low-conductivity strata

Earlier, we noted that in semi-thermal regions there are two possible reasons for above-average geothermal gradients: (a) the top few kilometres of crust may have better insulating properties than average (sedimentary basins are ideal), and (b) the upper crust may contain significant concentrations of heat-producing radioactive elements. This Section examines the first of these characteristics with particular reference to developments in the Paris area. In this type of non-volcanic geothermal system, heat is extracted faster than it is replaced; it is therefore a non-renewable energy resource — heat energy is being 'mined'.

Beneath the city of Paris and the surrounding area lies a large basin 500 km wide and 1–2 km deep, of Mesozoic (Triassic to Cretaceous) sedimentary rocks, some of which are important aquifers. Beds of coarse-grained porous limestones and sandstones alternate with impermeable clays, shales and marls (calcareous clays), as shown schematically in Figure 31.

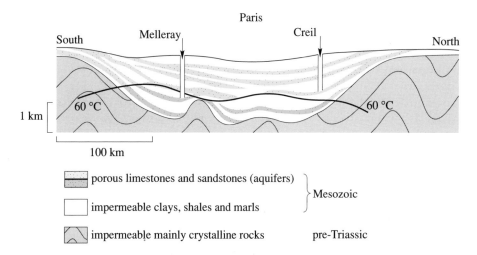

Figure 31 Cross-section through the Paris Basin showing the approximate positions of buried aquifers (colour) which alternate with less permeable, insulating layers of clay-rich sedimentary rocks. The 60 °C isotherm is marked, and the approximate positions of the two geothermal installations discussed in the text are also indicated.

○ Apart from its impermeable nature, in what other way is the clay–shale–marl group important geothermally?

○ The layers of coarser grained limestone and sandstone act as aquifers and carry meteoric water to depth where it is heated by a combination of the geothermal gradient and the insulating effects of the overlying low conductivity strata, the shales, which also seal water into the aquifers.

One reason why the French took the lead in developing the technique of exploiting geothermal heat from sedimentary basins was because the geology of the Paris Basin was already well known from the many oil exploration boreholes that had been drilled. Success with geothermal heating in this sedimentary basin has led to interest elsewhere, particularly in European countries where exploration for sites with suitable geological characteristics is well advanced. In the UK attention has focused on two

Plant design in the Paris area

Each plant uses water at between 55 and 70 °C which either rises under the natural head of *potentiometric pressure* or is pumped, from 1–2 km depth. The hot water is highly saline and too corrosive to be allowed directly into heating systems, so it is passed through corrosion-resistant heat exchangers. Here the geothermal heat is transferred to freshwater circulation systems connected to the distribution circuit. The distribution system in the vast greenhouse complex at Melleray (near Orléans) consists of both aerial and undersoil pipes. In contrast, a typical domestic supply, as at Creil (near Paris), might comprise a combination of underfloor and radiator pipes installed in 3000–4000 apartments in large blocks of flats (Figure 32). After passing through the heat exchanger, the cooled saline water in the primary geothermal circuit, now at 20–25 °C, is reinjected into the aquifer, normally at a point about 1 km away from the production well. This maintains the pressure in the aquifer and minimizes pollution.

Twin production and reinjection borehole systems are planned on the basis of supplying 3–5 MW of heat energy (25–50 litres a second of hot water) over a lifetime of 30–50 years. After this time, the heat in the aquifer at the base of the production well would

be depleted and could take several hundred years to recover. Because the capital costs of a single installation are high (about £2.5–3 million), it is important to plan for a consistently high heat load during its lifetime. Overall, the economics of these schemes are marginal at times of low oil prices and high interest rates. However, they are producing a natural saving of over 200 000 tonnes of oil a year in an area which, as recently as the 1960s, had no obvious geothermal potential.

Several horticultural schemes (e.g. at Melleray) and district heating schemes (e.g. at Creil) came into operation in the late 1970s and by 1990 no less than 55 such schemes were operating in the Paris area.

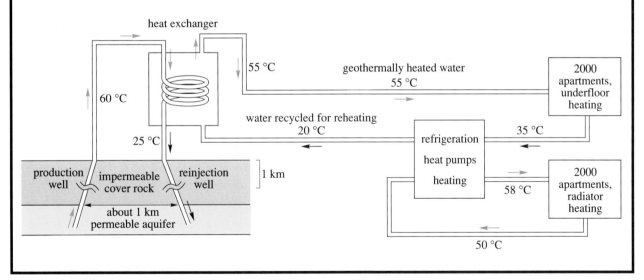

Figure 32 Simplified scheme of domestic or industrial space heating as used in the Paris area. On the left of the diagram, heat is exchanged between the geothermal water circuit and the secondary freshwater circuit. On the right, the water in the secondary circuit is used first to heat 2000 apartments by underfloor heating; the residual heat energy is then transferred to a smaller volume of water using heat pumps and is used for radiator heating in a further 2000 apartments.

deep basins, which also contain oil, centred on the Dorset–Hampshire and east Yorkshire–Lincolnshire areas. These are Mesozoic (Triassic to Cretaceous) basins containing a variety of sandstones and limestones which should have good porosity and permeability. There is also a cover of Tertiary sediments in the Hampshire area. The problem in the UK, where most households are heated independently, is one of finding places where the requirement is large enough to make exploitation realistic. Nevertheless, geothermal wells have been drilled to intersect Triassic sandstone aquifers, containing water at 71–76 °C, lying about 2 km below the Southampton area.

Geothermal heating in Southampton

A geothermal well in central Southampton was drilled by the Department of Energy in 1981 with an agreement that the City Council would develop an extensive district heating scheme if the well was successful. When only low flow rates could be obtained, this scheme was scaled down, and since 1989 the Civic Centre, Central Baths and several other buildings in a 2 km radius of the well (Figure 33) have been connected to hot water supplies using an underground pipe network. The scheme incorporates fossil fuel boilers which are run intermittently; maximum heat output is 12 MW of which 1 MW is supplied continuously from the geothermal source, which delivers 12 litres per second. This is considered a safe flow rate to secure a 20-year lifetime. A heat pump (see below) is soon to be introduced to reduce the brine discharge temperature and increase the geothermal input to 2 MW. A further technical aspect is the inclusion of a diesel generator supplying power to the various circulation pumps. Heat from the generator is fed into the district heating scheme and any surplus power is sold to Southern Electricity.

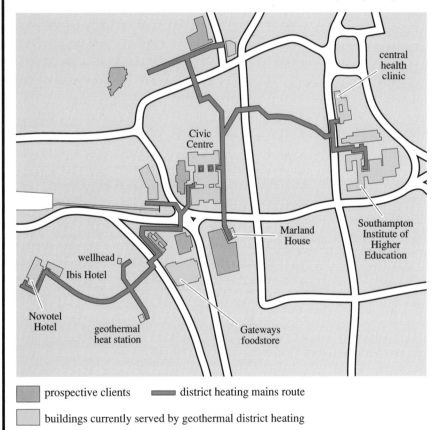

prospective clients   ▬ district heating mains route

buildings currently served by geothermal district heating

Figure 33   The Southampton geothermal district heating scheme: plant layout.

The Southampton Geothermal Heating Company, which now runs the operation, was charging the very modest sum of about 1 penny per kilowatt hour of heat consumed in the early 1990s. Neither the drilling nor the testing costs were met by the company, however, and the scheme was initially financed as a European Commission demonstration project. If the real costs of developing district heating schemes in the UK were absorbed then, depending on site conditions, the price would range up towards 5p per kilowatt hour. Arguably, this is marginal economics for a commercial concern, especially given the risk of drilling unsuccessful wells.

Finally, it is interesting to note the potential of heat pumps to enhance the efficiency of these geothermal systems. A *heat pump* performs the apparently magical task of taking thermal energy from a dilute source (e.g. a large volume of water at a low temperature) and concentrating it into a useful form (e.g. a small volume of water at a high temperature). Heat pumps are simply the more familiar air conditioner operating in reverse. In hot climates, air conditioners take heat from inside a building and dump it outside at a higher temperature whilst refrigerating the interior. The installation in Figure 32 uses geothermally heated water at 55 °C to supply underfloor heating to 2000 apartments, by which stage the water has cooled to 35 °C. Intermittent operation of heat pumps concentrates the energy from this water and transfers it to water in a separate circuit supplying radiator heating to a further 2000 apartments at 58 °C. The overall efficiency of the system is therefore critically dependent on the action of heat pumps to concentrate the remaining thermal energy after the first set of apartments has been heated.

In the longer term, heat pumps may allow the commercial development of shallower, cooler geothermal aquifers. The lower cost of drilling to shallower levels, combined with the widespread availability of shallow aquifers and the ability of heat pumps to produce small volumes of water at useful temperatures, is starting in some countries (notably Switzerland and France) to bring the cost of geothermal heating within range of small groups of, or even individual, dwellings. Clearly, owing to the nature of housing developments, this could enhance the prospects for geothermal district heating schemes in the UK.

3.3 Hot dry rocks

Beneath the granite moorlands of south-west England it is estimated that temperatures within granite intrusions may reach 220–240 °C at just 6 km depth (Figure 34). The granites are 270 Ma old, so these high temperatures are the result of radioactive decay rather than of magmatic heat. Such temperatures are interesting because of their potential for raising steam to drive turbines and produce electricity. South-west England is typical of several regions where above-average heat flow testifies to considerable geothermal energy resources in hot dry rocks (HDR) that lie within the range of deep drilling. The problem is that, whilst these rocks are *hot* because of their radioactive heat production, they are also *dry* because they are impermeable, and so are unable to carry a working geothermal fluid by which their heat content can be exploited.

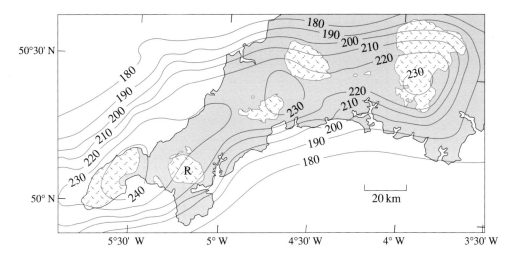

Figure 34   Projected temperature (°C) at 6 km depth beneath south-west England. Granite bodies that crop out at the surface are shown in colour. R = Rosemanowes quarry, site of the Camborne School of Mines HDR experiments.

The principle involves an injection well to carry water into the HDR zone where it circulates under pressure to a production well, and returns to the surface where it can be flashed to steam for electricity generation. The concept is much simpler to state than to bring into practice for, despite the investment of some $250 million, principally in the USA, UK, Germany and Japan, we are still some way from bringing a commercial HDR plant on line. The principal cost is drilling wells in hard crystalline rocks at high temperatures and under higher stresses (at 3–6 km depth) than in hyperthermal areas. However, this is proving much less difficult than the creation of an efficient circulation system to provide satisfactory heat exchange at depth.

HDR technology

The first experiments were initiated in the mid-1970s by the Los Alamos Scientific Laboratory (LASL) in New Mexico, USA. The approach was to pump water through a deep borehole at progressively increasing pressures until the rock above split to form a narrow vertical crack. This technique is used in the oil industry and is known as *hydrofracturing*. A second borehole is drilled to intersect the crack several hundred metres above its base; a closed circuit for water circulation through the fracture is thereby generated. The main problem with this technique is that hydrofracturing produces just a *single* crack through which all the water must pass; the surrounding rock therefore cools too rapidly. Nevertheless LASL ran an experimental binary cycle plant using this technology for more than a year. Of course, New Mexico has the advantage of being a semi-thermal region with some active volcanoes; it therefore has a higher geothermal gradient (about $60\,\text{K km}^{-1}$) than in the granites of south-west England (about $37\,\text{K km}^{-1}$).

If we assume that HDR fluids at temperatures of 150 °C could be exploited using binary cycle technology (Figure 29c), the minimum depth to which we would have to drill at the LASL site (New Mexico), assuming a mean surface temperature of 20 °C, would be:

$$(150 - 20)/60 \approx 2.2 \text{ km}$$

This also assumes negligible heat losses during ascent of the fluid.

Question 12

Making the same assumption, but using a surface temperature of 10 °C, what would be the minimum depth in south-west England?

During the 1980s much research has focused on developing rock fracture technologies, principally at LASL and at a Camborne School of Mines site, the Rosemanowes quarry, Cornwall (Figure 34). Here the aim has been to deviate twin boreholes at depth by up to 35° from the vertical, so that they intersect *natural* joints and fissures, leaving a vertical spacing of several hundred metres between them (Figure 35). Where necessary, small explosive charges may then be detonated in the lower hole to initiate a *multiple* fracture system and gain access to the main fissures which occur with an average 20 m spacing in Cornwall. The key stage of stimulating permeability in the rocks then involves pumping large volumes of water or low-viscosity gel, via the lower section of the injection well, at a pressure high enough to develop the required permeability between the two wells for long-term heat extraction. Using this approach, hydraulic connections at about 4 km depth beneath the LASL site, and at 2.6 km depth beneath Rosemanowes (half production depth) were successfully established.

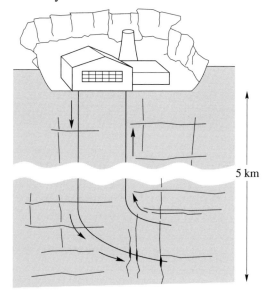

5 km

Figure 35 Conceptual model of a hot dry rock circulation system in which wells are developed from boreholes deviated to intersect the natural fracture systems of crystalline rocks. The heat exchange surface, or artificial reservoir created at depth, ideally consists of multiple fluid pathways between the injection (lower) and production (upper) wells. The separation between these wells would be about 300 m in Cornwall.

Numerous technical difficulties have been encountered during tests on experimental HDR systems, not least among which is the large diffusive losses of water that occur, much greater than the design loss of 10%. Plans to attract substantial European Commission funding to develop a single commercial prototype plant at one of three experimental European sites (Soultz in the Alsace area of France, Urach in the German Rhineland and Rosemanowes in Cornwall) were proposed in the early 1990s. However, cost projections were high and estimates for HDR electricity production have ranged from an optimistic 12p up to 35p per kWh. The economics are at best *extremely* marginal, and in fact the British HDR project was closed down in 1994 on economic grounds, though research at the French and German sites continued.

3.4 Summary of Section 3

1 Traditionally, 'renewable' geothermal energy has been exploited by drilling wells into high temperature aquifers from which steam can be produced at pressures of a few tens of atmospheres. Steam-dominated systems in hyperthermal volcanic areas are generally most efficient and economic, though water-dominated systems and, increasingly, cooler geothermal fluids on the flanks of hyperthermal areas are used for power generation.

2 Electricity generation from hyperthermal areas was about 5.8 GW in the early 1990s with a further 4.1 GW equivalent coming from direct uses of geothermal energy (steam and hot water). Geothermal power currently represents about 0.3% of the world's electrical needs, a figure that could grow to a few per cent in the next few decades, especially if the relatively non-polluting nature of geothermal technology becomes an important factor.

3 Geothermal resources in non-thermal areas include hot water, used for domestic and industrial space heating etc., which is pumped from aquifers in sedimentary basins, where temperature gradients are enhanced owing to the presence of low conductivity rocks in the sedimentary sequence. Twin production and reinjection wells are used to 'mine' the heat and a single system (as in the Paris Basin area) is designed to supply a heat load, typically with 3–5 MW of heat energy over 30–50 years.

4 Hot dry rock geothermal resources depend on extracting the energy from granite areas by the creation of an artificial aquifer. HDR technology has been the subject of much recent research and development, but has yet to be perfected to the point where these systems look attractive economically. Key aspects to be investigated are the stimulation of good long-term heat transfer surfaces underground and the reduction of water losses.

Question 13

Match each of the statements and predictions A–I with the most appropriate type (or types) of geothermal energy resource (1–3).

1 hyperthermal resources

2 sedimentary basins with low conductivity strata

3 hot dry rocks

A A non-renewable resource on the scale of human lifetimes.

B Suitable for electrical power generation.

C Requires artificial stimulation before energy can be tapped.

D Most suitable for domestic and industrial space heating.

E Productive aquifers require impermeable seal.

F Relies on extra heat produced by crustal rocks rich in radioactive elements.

G Relies on extra heat produced locally by recent magmatic activity.

H Potentially the most prolific geothermal resource for the foreseeable future.

I An internal energy resource.

4 SURFACE ENERGY RESOURCES

In this Section we consider renewable energy resources available at the Earth's surface, as summarized in the first Chapter of Block 4 *Energy 1*, i.e. those that depend on solar radiation alone (solar and biomass energy), or in combination with the Earth's rotation or gravity field (wind, wave and hydroelectric energy), or on the gravitational effect of the Sun and Moon (tidal energy).

It should be clear by now that reserves of fossil and nuclear fuels are sufficiently abundant to fulfil global energy requirements for the next few decades at least. However, several forms of renewable energy (including hyperthermal geothermal resources) are likely to play an increasingly important role in reducing the demand for these non-renewable fuels.

Many renewable forms of surface energy, often termed 'alternative energy resources', have been used in various forms for centuries. For example, the *kinetic energy* of moving air and water has been harnessed throughout much of recorded history. At their peak, there were probably 20 000 water mills operating in Britain for milling, grinding, weaving, and so on, and windmills were a feature of the agricultural landscape for many generations. But unlike fossil fuels, these energy sources are not transportable and were available for use only near the place of conversion. Also, they are mainly fluctuating energy sources, either because of diurnal variations (solar and tidal energy), or because of irregular fluctuations (wind, waves, etc.).

Among the most predictable sources are hydropower (Section 4.3), which already provides about 6% of global energy supply, and tidal energy (Section 4.4), which is generally seen as a natural extension of hydropower technology. The less predictable sources of wind and wave energy (Sections 4.2 and 4.5), especially wind energy, have recently received serious consideration in several countries. There is also considerable interest in developing techniques for converting solar energy into electricity and biomass into transportable fuels (Section 4.1).

4.1 Solar energy

At present, direct usage of solar energy contributes a negligible amount to world energy supply, yet only a small fraction of the incident solar radiation would need to be trapped in order to satisfy total demand.

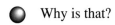 Why is that?

○ The Earth's surface receives some 10^{17} W of solar radiation, whereas the total global demand for energy of all kinds is about four orders of magnitude less than this, at around 10^{13} W.

However, as we saw in Block 4 *Energy 1*, the Earth's large surface area means that solar radiation is rather a 'dilute' energy source. It is also rather unevenly distributed: low latitudes (where the Sun is higher in the sky more of the time) receive more than high latitudes, and seasonal differences are smaller there too. Table 5 illustrates these points very well, comparing solar radiation for the British Isles with that for five other countries that have active solar energy programmes.

Table 5 Solar input statistics for various countries

Country	Energy input (10^6 J m^{-2} day^{-1})		
	Midsummer	Midwinter	Annual mean
United Kingdom	18	1.7	8.9
Ireland	18	2.1	10
Japan	17	7.0	13
USA	26	11	19
Australia	23	13	20
India	26	14	20
Israel	31	11	22

Low latitudes receive daily an average of about 20×10^6 J m^{-2} from the Sun, according to Table 5. How big an area is needed to receive the same amount of energy from the Sun in a day, as is available from a tonne of coal with a calorific value of 28×10^9 J?

We would need an area of:

$$\frac{28 \times 10^9 \, \text{J}}{20 \times 10^6 \, \text{J m}^{-2}} = 1.4 \times 10^3 \, \text{m}^2$$

a square of more than 35 m on a side.

What is more, that power supply is only available during daylight hours and it is greatly attenuated by cloud.

The intermittent dispersed and seasonal nature of solar radiation makes recovery difficult and expensive, particularly in the UK and other temperate lands, where it is especially 'dilute' (Table 5). The generally low efficiency of solar conversion panels greatly increases the area of collection required, and because solar energy peaks in summer, when demand is generally lowest, long-term storage is required. Conversion to electrical power is possible, but has all the drawbacks of a fluctuating energy source.

Methods of solar energy conversion are summarized in Figure 36. The following Sections provide a brief description of each technique and summarize its application on a world scale.

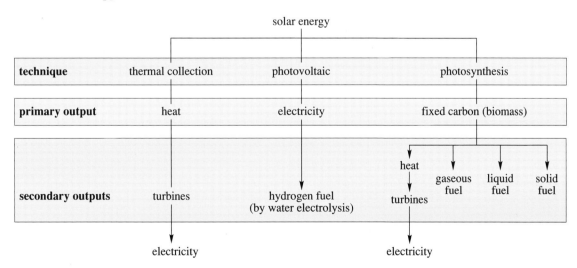

Figure 36 The three principal routes in the exploitation of solar energy.

4.1.1 Thermal collection of solar energy

Thermal collectors are of two main types: (a) flat-plate collectors, which are used to provide heat only (see Figure 36) for domestic and industrial water and space heating; and (b) focusing collectors, which are used to operate solar furnaces at high temperatures for electrical power generation.

Flat-plate collectors

You only have to visit an unventilated greenhouse on a sunny afternoon to appreciate that most buildings with glazed windows absorb solar energy. The interception of solar energy may be maximized (and radiation and other heat losses minimized) by improving the absorptive properties of the collector and by orienting it at the most effective angle to the Sun. Collectors therefore usually incorporate a glazed surface underlain by copper or aluminium tubes filled with air or water, which are connected to a system for water or space heating (Plate 47).

Design studies and practical applications have shown that a 1 m^2 solar collector panel has an average output of 1.3×10^9 J y^{-1} and that, for a typical house, 4–5 m^2 of panels are required for water heating. A much larger area would be required to produce enough energy for space heating: about 40 m^2, equivalent to all the south-facing or north-facing roof area of a typical house in temperate latitudes. Nevertheless, since domestic space heating accounts for nearly 20% of total energy demand in temperate latitudes, the potential savings are enormous. But there are two snags: (1) the large capital cost of solar collectors (about £300 m^{-2} in the early 1990s); and (2) the problem of energy storage from the period of peak summer input to the peak winter demand. Some ingenious solutions have been devised, such as storing the heat in underground water tanks or rock stores.

Focusing collectors

These are designed to concentrate the available solar energy to produce a secondary output at high temperature (Figure 36) for power generation. Early designs used arrays of sun-tracking mirrors (heliostats) focused on a solar furnace where temperatures of a thousand degrees centigrade or more could be achieved. Superheated steam produced in the furnace was forced through a generating turbine and then condensed to water for recycling (Figure 37).

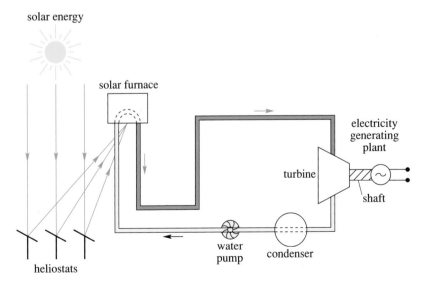

Figure 37 The operation of a heliostat-solar furnace power plant, such as that at Adrano, Sicily.

Technical problems with direct steam conversion led to more modern designs in which parabolic mirrors focus the Sun's rays onto pipes containing a high boiling point heat transfer liquid, which passes through heat exchangers to raise steam for the turbines (Plate 48).

Numerous experimental solar power stations with different design features have been developed in the south-western USA and western Europe, e.g. at Odeillo in the French Pyrenees and at Adrano, Sicily. They generate relatively small amounts of electricity compared with fossil fuel and nuclear stations — 1 MW at Odeillo, up to 80 MW in southern California. To make a significant contribution of, say, 1000 MW (3.15×10^{16} J y^{-1}), the incident solar energy over an area of about 18 km^2 would need to be collected and focused (assuming a conversion efficiency of 25–35%). This estimate is based on the optimum conditions near El Paso in the sunny south-western desert of the USA. Even in this location a 40% contribution from fossil fuel boilers would be needed to produce 1000 MW continuously, because the Sun does not shine at night and there are occasional cloudy days.

Although there is no shortage of land in the USA for developing solar power stations of this kind, capital costs are considerable because of the demand for large amounts of aluminium and steel (used in reflectors and their mountings), and the electricity generated is likely to cost more than from most other sources. Focusing collectors may become increasingly used in low-latitude countries, but they are unlikely to make a major impact on global energy supply.

4.1.2 Photovoltaic conversion of solar energy

The idea of using a light-sensitive **solar cell** is that it should convert *sunlight*, rather than heat, directly into electricity. The first low-efficiency photovoltaic cells using cuprous oxide on copper were developed for photographic exposure meters before 1940. During the 1950s the Bell Telephone Company introduced a silicon-based cell with a conversion efficiency of 11%. The basic principle is that a cell consists of flat sheets of two types of silicon (with different impurity elements) mounted one on top of the other, and when sunlight falls on the top sheet a current flows between the two. The most efficient solar cells are made with crystalline silicon and have a conversion efficiency of up to 15%, but they are relatively expensive. Much cheaper cells are made using amorphous (finely divided non-crystalline) silicon, but their efficiency is less — up to only about 5%.

In ideal conditions an *average* output of solar cells of around 30 Wm^{-2} (or 30 MW km^{-2}) could be expected on a daily basis and including seasonal variations. To generate 1000 MW using solar cells would require, therefore, 33 km^2 of land, an area similar to that for the solar furnace (which requires about 18 km^2 to produce 60% of 1000 MW), and a 'conventional' back-up would still be needed for night-time and cloudy days.

⬤ Can you think of any other problems that might inhibit the widespread large-scale commercial development of solar cells?

◯ Apart from the land requirements, the main problems are those of energy storage, the cost of fabricating large numbers of solar cells, and (the 'Achille's heel' of large-scale photovoltaics) the need for *inverters* to turn the direct current (DC) produced by the cells into alternating current (AC) for the grid system.

Even though developments in cell technology and improved methods of production have substantially reduced unit costs, large-scale photovoltaic conversion of solar energy is not likely to be economic for the foreseeable future. In the long term, electrolytic dissociation of water to produce hydrogen for fuel (Figure 36) may offer an appropriate storage method (see Section 5.2).

In the meantime, however, the reduction in unit costs of manufacturing the cells (by a factor of about ten in real terms since the early 1970s) has encouraged the widespread proliferation of this technology in small-scale applications. Many people are familiar with the extensive use of photovoltaics for auxiliary power and communications on rockets and space vehicles, with spin-offs into other small-scale uses such as solar-powered watches, calculators, battery chargers, and lightweight vehicles (Plate 49).

Since the late 1980s, photovoltaic cells have become an increasingly familiar feature in remote rural and mountainous locations, where it is impracticable and/or uneconomic to supply mains electricity or diesel generators (which require fuel to be brought in at regular intervals). Batteries and inverters (to convert DC to AC) enable the electricity to be used to drive low-voltage appliances (pumps, refrigerators and so on), with flat-plate collectors for water heating, whole communities can be self-sufficient in energy. The fuel is free (and electricity is generated even if there is cloud cover, though output is of course reduced), there are no moving parts and all that is needed is to keep batteries topped up and collecting surfaces clean.

Small photovoltaic systems designed to service single households also have enormous potential in developing countries, where mains electricity is often either unreliable or simply not available to the majority of the population (Plate 50). Trial experiments in Sri Lanka, Zimbabwe and the Dominican Republic, to name but three, have shown great promise for significantly increasing the standard of living of the people.

4.1.3 Energy from biomass

Through the photosynthetic fixation of carbon in plants, the Sun provides the energy for all processes in the biosphere. The chemical energy content of plants can be recovered as 'food' energy in the metabolism of animals, or as 'heat' energy in the combustion of biomass materials, e.g. wood, straw, plant matter and other waste organic materials. The process of growing and harvesting energy crops that have trapped solar energy by photosynthesis provides a third important method of harnessing solar energy (Figure 36).

● What advantages do you think biomass energy has over the other, more direct methods of solar energy conversion considered above?

○ One important advantage is that photosynthesis does not require bright sunlight but continues at a slow and steady rate even if the intensity of sunlight is very low. This means that 'energy crops' could be grown almost anywhere on the Earth's surface, though there would be some degree of competition with food crops.

The second advantage of biomass energy is that it can be converted into easily transported fuels, as indicated in Figure 36 and summarized below. But why *convert* it into fuels; what is wrong with using biomass materials themselves as fuels? Nothing at all. Indeed, wood is humanity's oldest energy source and it is still the principal fuel in many parts of the world, providing as much as 80% of the energy requirements of some developing countries (where the needs of growing populations can denude large areas of trees). Largely because of this, biomass (principally wood) accounts for about 15% of the world's commercial fuel consumption. In a number of countries small electricity generating plants, producing up to 30–40 MW, are fuelled by biomass — commonly wood chips, but including waste materials such as walnut shells and straw.

Question 14

Can you suggest one possible disadvantage and one (environmental) advantage of using wood, straw, vegetable matter, plant materials, etc., instead of coal and oil, say, for raising steam in power stations?

Despite the problems discussed in the answer to Question 14, biomass is incinerated for its energy content in many parts of the world: the potential of biomass, not only for combustion but also for conversion into more concentrated fuels, is becoming increasingly recognized. Conversion of biomass into other fuels must involve one of the following processes:

1   Controlled burning produces **biogas**, a mixture of methane and carbon dioxide, with a calorific value of around 16 MJ m^{-3} (compare with natural gas, about 43 MJ m^{-3}).

2   **Pyrolysis** (in which organic molecules are strongly heated in the absence of oxygen) yields solid, liquid and gaseous hydrocarbons. The solid fuel produced in pyrolysis, known as *char*, is a carbon-rich substance which has a high calorific value and can be formed into briquettes.

3   Digestion by bacteria in *anaerobic conditions* also produces biogas.

4   Anaerobic *glycolysis* (fermentation) or chemical reduction (in which the organic polymers are broken down) produces liquid alcohols and even hydrocarbon molecules like those in crude oil.

The main advantage of producing such concentrated fuels is that, like conventional hydrocarbon resources, they can be stored indefinitely. Apart from power generation, the main applications of gaseous and solid fuels would be in domestic and industrial space heating and thermally based manufacturing processes. The main potential use of liquid fuels would be in transport; for example, since the late 1970s a large part of the Brazilian sugar crop has been used to manufacture *ethanol*, which is added in a 1 : 3 ratio to petrol for some cars and trucks. These developments have required relatively small modifications to engine designs. The main practical disadvantages are that ethanol has a lower calorific value than petroleum (26 MJ kg^{-1} as against 44 MJ kg^{-1}) and is more expensive to produce. Moreover, in Brazil there have been worries about the progressive depletion of food crops in favour of the manufacture of alcohol fuels.

On a world scale, there should be no shortage of potentially available biomass energy. The equivalent of 10^{22} J y^{-1} is created annually by photosynthesis, whereas global energy demand is only about 3.5 $\times$ 10^{20} J y^{-1} (or 3.9 $\times$ 10^{20} J y^{-1} if the subsistence use of biomass, mainly wood, is included).

Energy from rubbish

About 70–80% of domestic rubbish consists of paper, card and other organic matter, all of which are potential sources of biomass energy. Some 20–30 million tonnes of such rubbish are produced annually in Britain alone, along with around twice as much again of combined industrial, commercial and agricultural wastes with a similarly high organic content. So, generating energy from refuse is an attractive option, not least because of the growing shortage of nearby landfill sites and high costs of transportation to more distant locations.

In several European countries as much as 30–40% of domestic refuse is incinerated (compared with less than 10% in the UK). The heat energy can be recovered for district heating or electricity generation (it is said that a third of the heating requirements of Paris are supplied in this way), and the ash can be used for construction and road building. Emission of dust, acids, metals and organic compounds (e.g. dioxins) is tightly controlled by environmental legislation.

Where landfill sites for rubbish disposal are available, however, extraction of biogas from decaying organic matter is an economic proposition. In the early 1990s there were already more than 240 commercial *landfill gas* schemes operating worldwide, with a total installed generating capacity of 440 MW, and there are countless smaller schemes in agricultural areas (in both developed and developing countries, e.g. India) making use of biogas from animal wastes. The gas is burned to fire kilns, furnaces or boilers, and to generate electricity for sale (Figure 38), or it can be liquefied under pressure for use as fuel for vehicles — some local councils in the UK run their vans and trucks on landfill gas. It is estimated that to make generation of landfill gas an economic proposition in the UK, a site should contain a minimum of 100 000 t of suitable refuse.

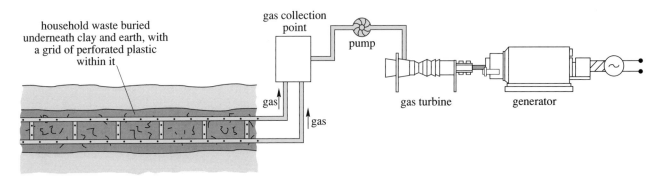

Figure 38 Extraction and use of landfill gas for electricity generation. The gas is used as fuel to drive a gas turbine engine, which in turn drives a generator.

Question 15

Which, if any, of the four conversion processes listed above (controlled burning, pyrolysis, digestion in anaerobic conditions, glycolysis) is being used in (a) incineration of domestic rubbish; (b) production of landfill gas?

The formation of biogas (including landfill gas) involves exactly the same chemical reactions as those which generate methane and the other hydrocarbon gases associated with coal and petroleum. Methane is a more powerful greenhouse gas than CO_2, and any that gets into the atmosphere unburnt will contribute to global warming. However, much of it undergoes natural photochemical oxidation to CO_2. This CO_2, plus any which occurs in the biogas itself (see earlier), is 'new' CO_2 (as opposed to 'fossil' CO_2) from trees, crops and so on, which is recycled back into the biosphere and so makes no contribution to global warming (see answer to Question 14).

4.2 Wind energy

Atmospheric circulation of air masses depends on two things: (a) differences in incident solar energy over the Earth's surface, which bring about variation in air density, causing winds to blow; (b) the gravitational and rotational energy of the Earth, which controls and modifies circulation patterns. The total amount of energy involved is about 3×10^{23} J y^{-1} but only a tiny fraction of this (about a quarter of 1%) can be tapped by windmills which are at most a few tens of metres high.

○ How do variations in wind speed affect the power generated by a windmill?

○ The kinetic energy of the wind is proportional to the square of its speed (v):

$$\text{kinetic energy} = \tfrac{1}{2}mv^2 \tag{4.1}$$

where a mass (m) of air passes a given area per second. In the case of windmill blades sweeping an area (A):

$$\text{mass per second } (m) = \text{density of air } (\rho) \times \text{swept area}$$
$$(A) \times \text{wind speed } (v) \tag{4.2}$$

The kinetic energy of the wind is partly transformed into pressure against the blades as the air is slowed down in passing through the area swept by the rotating blades. The power available to the windmill is given by combining Equations 4.1 and 4.2.

$$\text{kinetic energy per second (i.e. power)} = \tfrac{1}{2}(\rho Av)v^2$$

$$= \tfrac{1}{2}\rho Av^3 \tag{4.3}$$

Of course, it is not possible to extract all the energy in the wind since to do so would mean that the air would be brought to rest. However, a modern *turbine generator* attached to the axis of a windmill can recover about 80% of the available power. Most wind turbines operate only within a given range of wind speeds — a certain minimum speed is needed to start the blades rotating and, at the other end of the range, the blades are progressively 'feathered' (i.e. their effective area is reduced by angling them out of the wind direction) as the wind becomes stronger.

Question 16

The power available to a windmill from the wind is given by:

$\tfrac{1}{2}\rho Av^3$ (Equation 4.3)

A typical modern wind turbine has blades with an effective surface area (A) of 300 m^2 at a constant wind speed (v) of 10 m s^{-1} (23 m.p.h.). If the generator has an efficiency of 80%, determine its power output under these conditions, given density of air (ρ) = 1.3 kg m^{-3}. Note that your answer will be in watts. The units in Equation 4.3 multiply out to kg m^2 s^{-3}, which is the watt in basic SI units.

● If the wind speed given in Question 16 were to double, what would happen to the power output?

○ Because of the cube relationship between power output and wind speed, if wind speed doubles, power output increases by $(2)^3 = 8$ times, and the generator would be putting out 8×150 kW = 1.2 MW.

Two main designs of wind turbine have been developed, both of which range up to several megawatts output. The more traditional (Figure 39a) has a horizontal axis of rotation and the generator is mounted either with the rotor at the top of the tower (as shown) or at the foot of the tower, linked to the rotor by a right-angle drive and vertical shaft. The perennial problem of keeping the rotor facing into the wind has led to the development of vertical-axis machines (Figure 39b) arranged around a vertical shaft which drives a ground-based generator. However, these are not yet economically competitive with the more traditional types.

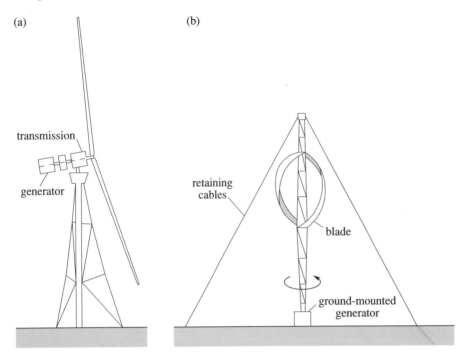

(a)

(b)

transmission

generator

retaining cables

blade

ground-mounted generator

Figure 39 Wind-powered generators with (a) horizontal and (b) vertical axes. (Note: The 'twist' shown in the blades in (b) is greatly exaggerated.) Horizontal axis generators are commonly three-bladed, and vertical axis types can also have 'H' or 'V' shaped arrangement of blades.

Unlike solar energy, wind movements in temperate latitudes are strongest during winter months at the time of peak demand for energy. However, wind is still unpredictable and back-up or storage facility is needed for windless periods.

Nevertheless, wind power has become one of the front-runners among alternative energy options, especially in Denmark, which lacks fossil fuels and has a history of research and development into electricity from wind power going back to the nineteenth century. In the early 1990s, Denmark had installed more than 3000 wind turbines with over 350 MW total capacity.

California is another region where wind energy has a high profile, although large-scale installation of wind farms there dates only from about the 1980s. By the early 1990s, however, around 15 500 wind turbines were operating in California, representing over 1600 MW of generating capacity (Plate 51).

Commercial development of wind energy began in the UK during the 1970s and grew slowly through the 1980s, with one-off individual installations, ranging in output from 200–250 kW up to 3–4 MW, in places such as the Orkneys and Carmarthen Bay. The first commercial wind farm began supplying electricity to the grid in late 1991, at Delabole in Cornwall, using ten 400 kW turbines of 34 m diameter. Since then, other wind farms have been installed, e.g. near Cemaes Bay in Anglesey, on Ovenden Moor near Halifax, near Carmarthen in mid-Wales and near Blythe on the north-east coast. Costs have progressively decreased in the last couple of decades, and by the early 1990s wind power was competitive with other sources of electricity, at around 5p per kWh, with lifetimes of 30 years or so for the installations. The UK programme received a boost from the Non-Fossil Fuel

Obligation, which was introduced at the time of electricity privatization and required electricity companies to buy a proportion of their supply from non-fossil fuel sources (see Section 2.1.4). By the mid-1990s there were plans for major wind farm developments at several upland sites in the British Isles.

However, it must be borne in mind that several hundred huge wind machines spread over a large 'wind farm' area would be needed to replace just one 1000 MW coal-fired power station.

● Why is that?

○ The principal reason is that wind is a relatively 'dilute' energy source, on account of the low density of air. To generate 3 MW you need a wind turbine 75 m high, with a rotor diameter of 60 m (Figure 40) *and* a steady wind of around 15 m s^{-1} (more than 30 m.p.h.).

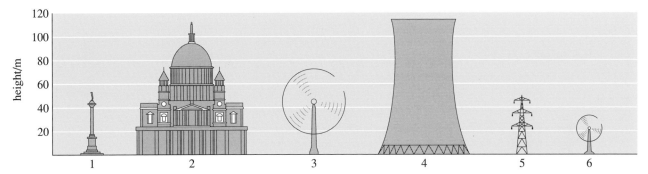

A 1000 MW 'wind farm' would need at least 350 such machines over a minimum area of 1–2 km^2 (compared with about 0.25 km^2 for a fossil fuel power station). On the other hand, the energy source is non-polluting, and the area between wind turbines can be cultivated or used to support livestock.

Figure 40 Comparison of the sizes of wind turbines with some other well-known landmarks: 1, Nelson's Column, 52 m; 2, St Paul's Cathedral, 111 m; 3, Orkney 3 MW wind turbine, 75 m; 4, coal-fired power station cooling tower, 114 m; 5, electricity grid pylon, 50 m; 6, Carmarthen Bay, 200 kW wind turbine, 35 m.

Nevertheless, construction and maintenance would be a major undertaking, there is loss of visual amenity, noise pollution could be a serious problem for some local residents, and power output would be zero on calm days. Such considerations formed the basis of protest movements in several parts of Britain, as more wind farm developments were planned in the mid-1990s. This contrasts significantly with the more relaxed attitude to the technology in Denmark, where the proportion of wind-generated electricity is much greater than in Britain. Danish wind-farm developments tend to be relatively small and are community-based, with local residents able to benefit directly from operation of the wind turbines in their area. In Britain, on the other hand, the best sites are in scenically attractive upland areas of low population density, and developments are relatively large. Local residents have felt that the wind farms were imposed on them from outside by large companies (with Government support), with little prior consultation and no involvement of the community.

4.3 Hydroelectric power

People have used the energy of running water for many centuries; indeed, water provided the main source of mechanical energy, chiefly through water wheels, until it was superseded by steam in the nineteenth century. Today, this renewable source of primary energy provides about 5–6% of world energy needs. Whether the energy is harnessed by a wooden wheel in a tiny stream in Nepal or by a 100-tonne dynamo (alternator) at Aswan on the Nile, all hydroelectric power generation (hydropower) originates from the *water cycle* of evaporation, precipitation and run-off, powered by the Sun's heat coupled with the Earth's gravity.

● What is the principal advantage of flowing water over moving air as means of power generation?

○ Water is very much denser than air so that, for a given speed, the kinetic energy is also much greater than for air — flowing water is a more concentrated form of energy.

The principle of hydroelectric power generation is very simple: water flowing down steep gradients is channelled through pipes and gives up its kinetic energy to rotating turbines which drive electrical generators. Modern hydroelectric turbines have efficiencies exceeding 90%, so most of the potential energy of water stored in a dammed reservoir can be converted into electricity.

The power developed depends on the product of the water discharge rate (Q, in $m^3 s^{-1}$) and the **working head** (the vertical fall of water flowing into the hydroelectric plant, H, in metres) as follows:

$$N = Kg\rho QH \tag{4.4}$$

where N is the power output in watts ($J s^{-1}$), g is the acceleration due to gravity, ρ is the density of water and K is the efficiency of the generating system involved. Clearly, installations that have a large working head require smaller discharge rates for equivalent power output than do those with a small working head, as in tidal barrage schemes (Section 4.4). Thus mountainous countries, such as Norway, Switzerland and New Zealand, can rely greatly on hydropower because working heads exceeding 1000 m are often available (Norway was self-sufficient in hydropower in the mid-1990s). However, most of the best sites for such installations have already been used in industrialized nations, and smaller installations, using heads of 20–30 m on broad rivers, have become economic (e.g. in Switzerland and Alpine France) as the cost of fossil fuel energy has risen.

Interest in smaller hydropower installations has increased in Britain too, often involving combined water management and power generation schemes, as at the Kielder reservoir in north-east England (Plate 32), where more than 6 MW is produced from 15 $m^3 s^{-1}$ of water discharge.

● Use Equation 4.4 to calculate the working head needed to generate 6 MW from a discharge of 15 $m^3 s^{-1}$. Assume a conversion efficiency of 90%, and make sure that your units balance, bearing in mind that the joule is the unit of energy, expressed in basic SI units as $J = kg\, m^2\, s^{-2}$.

○ Substituting numbers (and units) into Equation 4.4 ($N = Kg\rho QH$):

$$6 \times 10^6\ (J\,s^{-1}) = 0.9 \times 9.8\ (m\,s^{-2}) \times 10^3\ (kg\,m^{-3}) \times 15\ (m^3\,s^{-1}) \times H$$

So,

$$H = \frac{6 \times 10^6\ (J\,s^{-1})}{132.3 \times 10^3\ (m\,s^{-2} \times kg\,m^{-3} \times m^3\,s^{-1})}$$

$$= \frac{6 \times 10^3\ (J\,s^{-1})}{132.3\ (kg\,m\,s^{-2}\,s^{-1})}$$

$$= \frac{6 \times 10^3\ (kg\,m^2\,s^{-2}\,s^{-1})}{132.3\ (kg\,m\,s^{-2}\,s^{-1})}$$

$$= 45\ (m)$$

Another application of hydropower, which has been developed at several sites in Britain, is in **pumped storage schemes**, where the same water is recycled between two reservoirs at different altitudes (Figure 41).

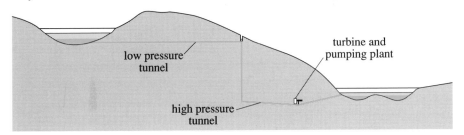

Figure 41 A cross-section of the Dinorwic pumped storage hydroelectric scheme at Llanberis, north Wales. The vertical shaft linking the low-pressure and high-pressure tunnels is 440 m deep and 10 m wide.

Low-cost electricity from other power stations, usually nuclear stations which are not easily closed down over short periods, is used during the night to pump water to the top reservoir. The process is reversed to generate electricity during periods of peak demand such as occur during winter evenings (Figure 42), especially just after popular TV programmes. The Dinorwic pumped storage scheme at Llanberis in North Wales, constructed in the 1970s to be linked with the nearby Trawsfynydd nuclear power station, is the largest such scheme in Britain: its maximum output of 1320 MW can be reached in 10 seconds during an emergency (Plate 52). The Trawsfynydd station developed structural problems in the late 1980s and was closed down in 1993 (Section 2.1.4).

Of course, pumped storage schemes are net consumers of electricity because it takes more energy to pump water to the top reservoir than is returned when the same amount of water is released through the turbines. However, this method of *storing* electrical energy represents an enormous saving in generating costs over alternative methods of meeting peak demand, which involve operating coal-fired or oil-fired stations well below their economic capacity for most of the time.

4.3.1 Contribution of hydropower to global power supplies

Figure 43 summarizes estimates of the world distribution of available and potential hydropower in the mid-1980s. The estimated total available potential has not changed much with time, and stands at about 2200 GW, whereas the total installed capacity has risen from some 350 GW in the mid-1970s to about 500 in the mid-1980s to over 600 GW by the early 1990s — around 6% of total world energy production, and nearly 20% of electrical energy production.

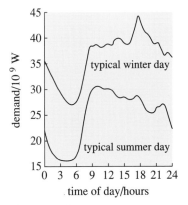

Figure 42 Daily summer and winter electrical power demand on the supply system in Britain. Note that the typical winter evening peak demand shown here is 45 GW: the highest peak demand made on the system is closer to 50 GW.

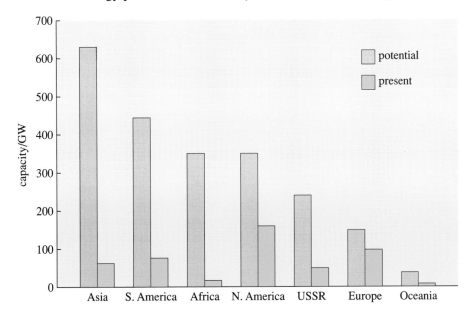

Figure 43 Estimated potential and actual world hydroelectric capacity, by region, for the mid-1980s.

The world's largest hydropower station uses a 7 km long dam across the
Paraná river at Itaipu on the Brazil–Paraguay border. It was opened in
November 1982, and was projected to have a generating capacity of
12 600 MW by the late 1980s, which Brazil found difficult to absorb, because
the demand for electricity had increased much more slowly than anticipated
when the scheme was planned in 1970. This is another example of how
political and economic factors can change radically during the long *lead
times* that are required in exploiting certain physical resources. Indeed, it has
been argued that large hydropower schemes are irrelevant to developing
countries, which may have little use for large amounts of electrical power.
The main beneficiaries of large hydropower schemes in the Third World are
commonly big industrial enterprises such as aluminium smelters, many of
which may be local outposts of multinational companies.

Question 17

(a) Why has development of potential hydropower resources proceeded
     much further in some continents that in others (Figure 43)?

(b) Bearing in mind the contrasted nature of the resources, how would you
     expect the global distribution of hydropower potential among different
     countries to differ from that of fossil fuels?

Growth of hydropower generation has more or less kept pace with, or
slightly exceeded, the growth in total world energy production, and may
continue to contribute between 5% and 10% of total demand. In Britain it
contributes about 2% of our electrical energy; there is little scope for further
development, except through installation of pumped storage schemes.

⬤ Despite the rather optimistic view of the global contribution of
   hydropower portrayed so far, there are some snags involved in
   damming major rivers — what might these be?

◯ There are many conflicting claims on suitable sites, such as irrigation,
   river navigation, flood control or fisheries. Another major problem is
   finance: although industrialized nations have assisted with projects such
   as the Aswan Dam in Egypt and the Kariba Dam in Zimbabwe, such
   large schemes are frequently beyond the resources of the developing
   nations to maintain, and even major reservoirs are likely to become silted
   up eventually. Both these African schemes suffered from yet another
   problem — the unexpected spread of disease resulting from the formation
   of large areas of open water where bacteria and mosquitoes breed.

It is often claimed that hydroelectric generation produces 'clean power', but
the environmental costs can be considerable, in part because of the conflicts
outlined above. For instance, the Hoover Dam greatly reduced downstream
flow in the Colorado River, and further abstraction of water along its length
has resulted in virtually zero flow at its mouth in the Gulf of California.

Another example is the Danube which is already used for hydroelectric
power generation at a number of sites. One such development is the major
dam completed in the early 1970s near Turnu-Severin, where the river
formed the border between Romania and what was then Yugoslavia. The
resulting lake, stretching some 80 km upstream, completely obliterated the
unique and spectacular Iron Gates gorge, famous for centuries as one of
Europe's most dramatic landscapes. While this has been deplored on
environmental grounds, the dam — said to be the tenth largest in the world —
provides some 10% of Romania's electricity needs.

Also on the Danube, a planned 880 MW installation on the Czech–Hungarian border was agreed in 1978 and included flood protection as well as two power stations, and involved diversion of the main flow over a distance of several hundred metres. The project excited much controversy, and in the late 1980s, concern on environmental as well as economic grounds, particularly on the part of Hungary, halted construction for an indefinite period. However, in 1992 the newly independent state of Slovakia (formerly eastern Czechoslovakia) went ahead with the diversion, chiefly on the grounds that the hydropower was urgently needed to supplement or replace electricity produced by old and inefficient coal-fired and nuclear plant. The Hungarians claimed it would greatly diminish both their surface and underground water supplies and reduce the width of the Danube from about 300 m to less than 50 m, but in the event it appears that these claims may have been exaggerated.

Most ambitious of all, in 1993 the Chinese Government gave approval for the first stage of a gigantic project to build the world's largest hydropower scheme by damming the Yangtse River just downstream of the historically famous and scenically spectacular Three Gorges. The statistics are awe-inspiring. The dam will be 175 m high and 2 km long, impounding some 40 km^3 of water in a lake 600 km long and up to 150 m deep. The cost is estimated at up to US $20 billion over 10–15 years and the power generated will be 17 000 MW, a third more than Brazil's Itaipu scheme. The scheme is intended also to provide river regulation and flood prevention, and navigation along this stretch of the river will be greatly improved. Not surprisingly, the plan attracted international protest as well as internal dissent, not least because over a million people will be displaced, 100 towns and villages submerged and over 4000 km^2 of land flooded (equivalent to a strip 7 km wide along the whole length of the lake), including of course most of the rugged scenery of the Gorges themselves, with irreversible effects on the local ecology and climate.

In general, we can say that the larger the dam, the bigger the investment, the more serious the social and environmental disruption, the longer the lead time, and the greater the danger that circumstances will change before the project is completed and make it redundant.

However (as with photovoltaics, Section 4.1.2), the potential for *small-scale* exploitation of hydropower is enormous. The energy of small rivers and streams can be harnessed almost anywhere, with minimal environmental impact, and would be especially useful in remote hilly mountainous regions where it is uneconomic to supply mains electricity or fuel for generators. Indeed, such 'micro-hydro' schemes were quite common in places like Wales, both before and just after the Second World War.

4.4 Tidal energy

The energy of the tides depends on the gravitational pull of the Moon, and to a lesser extent the Sun, acting on the oceans as they rotate with the Earth. The total amounts to 8×10^{19} J y^{-1}, but there are many practical reasons why only a small fraction of this can actually be exploited. Tidal mills, like water mills, have been used for centuries (Plate 53), and the use of tidal energy for electrical power generation is based on the same principles as the generation of hydroelectric power. A tidal scheme requires a large tidal basin, across which a long dam (known as a *tidal barrage*) can be built to trap the water introduced at high tides. The water levels between the two sides of the barrage are balanced by controlled flow through sluices and turbines set in the barrage.

● How will the relationship $N = KgrQH$ (Equation 4.4) between power production, discharge rate and working head apply to the tidal scheme?

○ The head (H) will vary constantly according to the state of the tide and, although the potential discharge rate (Q) is vast, flow can occur only during those periods when there is a significant difference in water level between the two sides of the barrage. Because the head (H) available in a tidal power scheme is always small (it cannot be more than about 15 m and is usually less), Q must be large to generate significant amounts of power (N), and conversion efficiencies are generally less than in conventional hydropower schemes.

Figure 44a illustrates a simple example in which water flows through the turbine on the ebb-tide only — this is called single direction generation. The variations in sea level outside and within the basin are shown, respectively, by black and coloured curves, and the coloured shading represents the height of the head when generation can occur. Cross-sections showing water levels and flow directions are given below the curves. Two periods of 4–5 hours a day only are available for power generation, assuming twice-daily (semi-diurnal) tides. Where tides are diurnal, a single 8–10 hour period per day is available for power generation. The daily output of a tidal scheme can, of course, be extended by using two-way (reversible) turbines with power generation on both the rising and falling tides (Figure 44b), known as double direction generation.

Question 18

(a) Compare Figures 44a and 44b. Roughly by how much would operating on both rising and falling tides extend the period available for power generation from each two-tide cycle of about 25 hours?

(b) Which of the following types of coastline would be most suitable for siting a tidal barrage power station and why?
1   coastline with cliffs exposed to storms;
2   low-lying coastline subjected to strong currents parallel to the shore;
3   broad estuary with high tidal ranges;
4   major delta system transporting large volumes of water and sediment to the sea.

Figure 44   The times at which tidal power generation is possible, assuming semi-diurnal tides. (a) Single direction generation on the ebb tide only. (b) Double direction generation on both the flood and ebb tides.

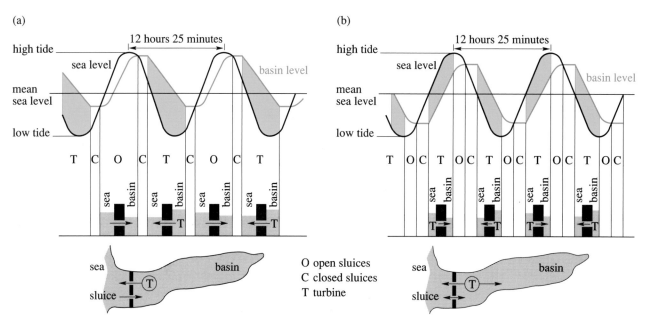

Although tidal power provides a diurnal output which is often out of phase with daily demand, it is a completely predictable and highly reliable source of renewable energy. This has been effectively demonstrated by a small experimental station near Murmansk in Russia, which was completed in 1979; by a 20 MW scheme in Nova Scotia, commissioned in 1984; and most significantly, by some 30 years of production from the 240 MW La Rance tidal station at St Malo in Brittany.

The main part of the La Rance dam contains twenty-four 10 MW turbines, which generate power in one direction only but which can be used in the opposite direction as pumps to increase the available head, rather like a pumped storage scheme (Plate 54). The minimum head at which the turbines produce maximum power output is 5.65 m, though they can operate with heads as low as 3 m. With an average tidal range of 8–9 m at La Rance, the equivalent of 5–6 hours a day at maximum output has been achieved, on average, since the equipment was installed (i.e. 240 MW for 5–6 hours per day, equivalent to 55 MW continuous power generation). In recent years, double-direction generation has been operated during spring tides, making it possible to produce power at maximum output for 7–8 hours per day. The local amenities have benefited in the form of improved agricultural and water management in the surrounding countryside, a motor road across the estuary along the barrage, and improved fishing and sailing facilities.

At prices obtaining in the early 1990s, a scheme of the type at La Rance would cost about £250 million, and produce electricity at 6–8 pence per kWh, taking into account the interest and depreciation, which is not very different from the cost of power from conventional sources. The main environmental cost is the need for dredging operations to avoid permanent silting up of the estuary. The main advantage is that tidal energy resources are renewable.

Good sites for tidal power schemes around the world are few, mainly because of the large tidal range required. The most interesting undeveloped sites are Canada's Bay of Fundy, which has the highest tidal range in the world (17 m) and the Severn estuary in the UK (Figure 45), where the funnelling effect of the coastline magnifies a normal tidal range of 4 m up to an average of 11 m between Cardiff and Weston-super-Mare.

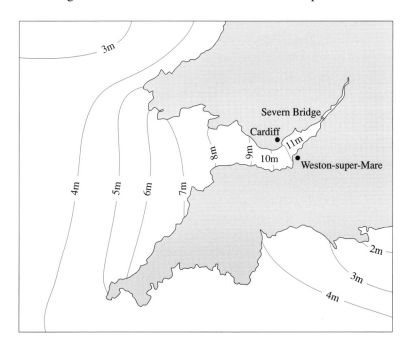

Figure 45 The average ranges (in metres) of spring tides in the Severn estuary and adjacent regions, showing how the tidal effect is amplified by the funnel-shaped channel.

The proposed Severn estuary barrage between these two towns would produce some thirty times more power than La Rance, because of the much larger water volumes and working head. The scheme would use between 160 and 200 turbines (Figure 46) each of between 36 and 45 MW maximum output (depending on the number), to give a total installed capacity of 7200 MW. The likely output, based on La Rance experience, would be equivalent to about 1500 MW continuous (about 5×10^{16} J y^{-1}), providing about 6% of UK *electrical* energy demand. The scheme would be kept as simple as possible with ebb-tide generation only; the extra cost of more complex schemes would not lead to proportional benefits in output.

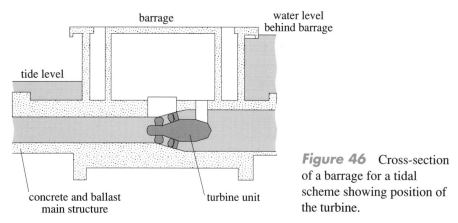

Figure 46 Cross-section of a barrage for a tidal scheme showing position of the turbine.

However, the environmental impact of barrage construction would be widespread, affecting not only local drainage but also aquatic and bird life, as well as amenity value. Sand, gravel and hard-rock blocks would be required in enormous amounts — some 40×10^6 m^3 of aggregates for the solid embankment alone, plus another 5×10^6 m^3 or so to build more than 100 hollow concrete structures equipped with sluices and turbines, each weighing 90 000 tonnes, which would be floated into position. The downstream side of the embankment would be constructed of coarse rock fragments sufficiently heavy to withstand currents when first dumped into the sea. This barrier would be backed by an upstream extension of lower grade materials (sand, mine waste, etc.) to provide mass and stability to the structure. Both surfaces, particularly the seaward surface, would then be protected from erosion by a layer of coarse hard-rock blocks (rip-rap); the barrage would be like an enormous dam, but with many more 'holes', and therefore much more costly.

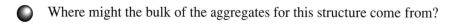

Where might the bulk of the aggregates for this structure come from?

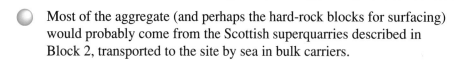

Most of the aggregate (and perhaps the hard-rock blocks for surfacing) would probably come from the Scottish superquarries described in Block 2, transported to the site by sea in bulk carriers.

Between the late 1970s and early 1990s, the UK Government and several private investors provided some £10 million to fund feasibility studies on the Severn Barrage, but implementation of the project would be extremely expensive: the estimated cost had risen to over £10 billion (compared with £6 billion a decade earlier), and construction would take around 10 years. Given this long lead time and huge scale of investment, it is perhaps not surprising that the Government has preferred to leave development of tidal barrages up to the private sector. Smaller barrage schemes could prove more attractive propositions, because of the proportionately lower capital costs. These include the Mersey in north-west England (700 MW installed; see Box 'The Mersey Barrage project'), Strangford Lough in Northern Ireland (200 MW installed), and other smaller estuaries, such as the Wyre and Conwy.

The Mersey Barrage project

The Mersey enjoys tides of up to 10 m range with a mean spring range of 8.4 m. After the Severn, this is the largest range in Britain, making it eminently suitable for power generation. Another advantage is that the broad upper estuary discharges into Liverpool Bay through a deep and narrow channel, which could be closed by a barrage of economical length, where the water depth is sufficient for suitably sized turbines and sluices to be installed. The barrage would impound an upstream basin of about 70 km², and it would be about 2 km long and 70 m wide, with a crest level similar to the existing riverside works: a road crossing could be incorporated, to ease city centre congestion.

Feasibility studies carried out since 1986 included: civil engineering design of all aspects of the Project; environmental impacts on feeding grounds of wading birds, particularly the sand and mud banks (Figure 47), the quality of the impounded water and sediments; and the effects on shipping.

It was planned to have 46 gated sluices in the barrage to allow the incoming tide to flow into the upper estuary, the area impounded by the barrage. Once the tide reached maximum height, and started to ebb, the sluice gates would be closed and the impounded water released through the turbines, which would generate up to 700 MW of electricity. There would be 28 turbine units each driving a 25 MW generator. The turbines are designed to have a secondary function of pumping at the top of the tide, to further increase the volume of impounded water and hence the net energy output. In order to maintain shipping access to and from upper reaches of the Mersey, two locks would be built, one on each side of the river. In the early 1990s the Mersey Barrage seemed the most likely of the UK tidal schemes to go ahead, at an estimated cost of about £1 billion. Most of this would be raised from private finance—£5 million or so had already been spent on feasibility studies, about half of it from Government funding. But the Government was apparently reluctant to commit more money to the scheme, and in 1993 the project was indefinitely postponed.

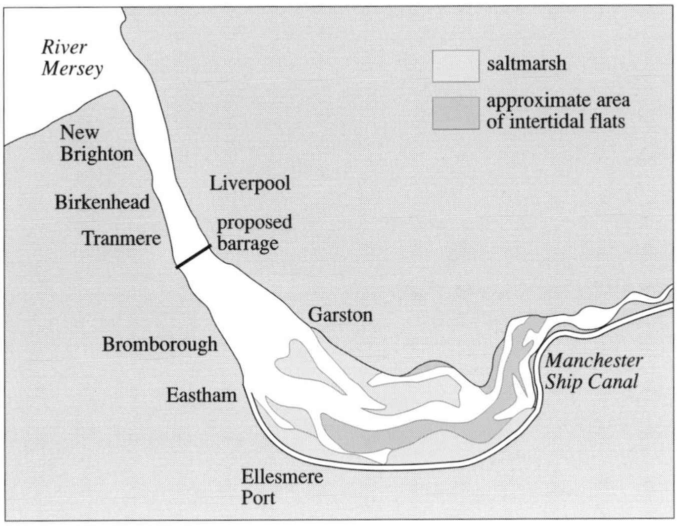

Figure 47 Location of the proposed Mersey Barrage.

Activity 2 Tidal and wind power compared

Tidal power is totally predictable, if intermittent, whereas wind power is not: the wind may not blow for days at a time, but the tides will rise and fall just the same. Moreover, moving air is a much more 'dilute' energy source than moving water, on account of its lower density.

Yet wind farms proliferate in several countries, and there is only one major tidal power station operating anywhere in the world: La Rance.

Why do you think this is? In your explanation you should consider: relative contribution to regional power supplies that can be expected from power stations 'fuelled' by wind and by tides; lead times; lifetimes; scale and timing of investment and return; resource requirements for construction; location and environmental factors.

You need also to know that capital costs per kilowatt of installed capacity are a little more than £1000 for tidal power and a little less than £1000 for wind power.

4.5 Wave energy

Waves are generated in the ocean by the action of winds blowing over the water, and so two main factors govern the amount of energy available from waves: the wind strength, and the uninterrupted distance they travel over the ocean, known as the *fetch*. The geographical location of the British Isles is ideal on both counts because they lie on one of the main global wind belts and receive waves from the long fetch of the North Atlantic. The energy of a wave is related to its *amplitude* (which is half the wave height from crest to trough), and the greater the wind speed and/or fetch, the greater the amplitude *(a)*. The total power *(P)* per unit length of wave front is given by:

$$P = \tfrac{1}{2}\rho gca^2 \text{ watts per metre} \tag{4.5}$$

where ρ is the density of water and c is the speed of the wave.

○ Use Equation 4.5 to calculate the power of waves with an amplitude of 1 m and a speed of $4\,\text{m s}^{-1}$, which is typical of waves that occur around the British coastline. What would happen to the power if the amplitude were increased to 5 m as in severe storm conditions? ($\rho = 10^3\,\text{kg m}^{-3}$; $g = 9.8\,\text{m s}^{-2}$)

○ Substituting in Equation 4.5, we have

$$P = \tfrac{1}{2} \times 10^3 \times 9.8 \times 4 \times 1^2 \text{ W m}^{-1}$$

$$= 19.6 \times 10^3 \text{ W m}^{-1}$$

$$\approx 20 \text{ kW m}^{-1}$$

The power is proportional to the square of the amplitude, so it would increase by a factor of 25 if the amplitude increased to 5 m, i.e. to $500\,\text{kW m}^{-1}$.

Figure 48 shows the most favoured sites for wave energy conversion around the British coastline where the power output normally approaches or exceeds that calculated above.

○ On Figure 48, directional 'roses' indicate the wave field at selected points. What is the average wave power off south-west England?

○ The average power level is between 35 and $42\,\text{kW m}^{-1}$, most of it arriving from a westerly or south-westerly direction.

Anyone who has watched storm waves battering a cliff cannot fail to be impressed by the potential of wave power. In fact, however, a wave front with a power of 40 kW per metre would need to be harnessed by converters, such as those in Figure 49, along a 50 km length to yield the power output of a large (1000 MW) coal-fired power station, assuming (somewhat optimistically) 50% efficiency. This would prove difficult for the following reasons:

(a) The average power density is low (50 km for 1000 MW), so a large capital investment is required for the converter system to produce a worthwhile output.

(b) The converter system must be built to cope with rapid short-term variations of power (from calm to storm in 24 hours or less), ranging up to a peak of 10 000 kW per metre, nearly three hundred times more powerful than the average.

45 kW m^{-1}

48 kW m^{-1}

25 kW m^{-1}

57 kW m^{-1}

14 kW m^{-1}

14 kW m^{-1}

42 kW m^{-1}

Scotland

42 kW m^{-1}

S.W. England

35 kW m^{-1}

(c) The power output would be as random and unpredictable as the weather, requiring either back-up systems or energy storage (batteries). Long (tens of kilometres) rows of converters would form offshore 'barrages', which could interfere with shipping, and problems (and costs) of maintenance would be formidable. More important perhaps, the more efficient the conversion, the calmer the water would become on the shoreward side.

Figure 48 Principal locations of wave power potential around the UK coastline. The heavy lines show the locations of the optimum wave power potential around the British Isles. Numbers are the estimated power availability in kilowatts per metre averaged over 12 months at the points shown. The directional 'roses' indicate the relative magnitudes of the directional components of the wave climate at the selected points.

 Why is that?

 Because, by analogy with wind energy, if most of the wave power is extracted, the wave amplitude must decrease (Equation 4.5).

The ecology of long stretches of coastline would be abruptly and dramatically changed; water circulation and sediment transport would decrease, the growth of quiet water organisms would increase, and pollutants would be less easily flushed out.

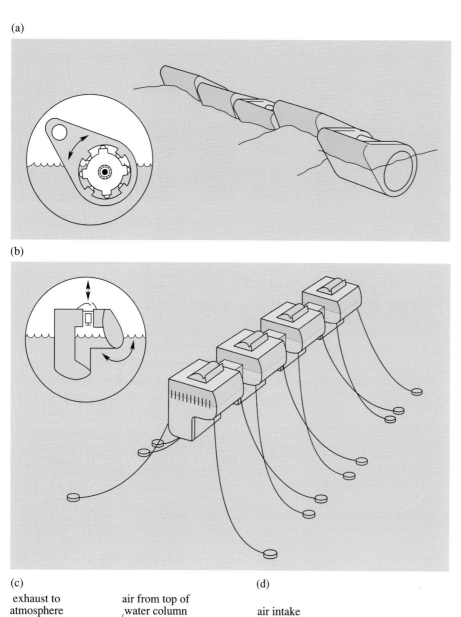

(a)

(b)

(c)

exhaust to
atmosphere

air from top of
water column

4 way
valve

incoming
wave

turbine

(d)

air intake

4 way
valve

outgoing
wave

turbine

Figure 49 Wave-energy converters. (a) The Salter duck. This device consists of an oscillating vane within a float that rocks up and down on a central spine, and can be used to drive generators. (b) An oscillating water column based on the 'inverted-can' principle: incoming waves set up oscillations of the air columns trapped in the inverted vessels; these oscillations can be used to drive turbines or a high-pressure fluid power system. Smaller devices using this principle are used for lighting systems on navigation buoys. (c) and (d) More details of an oscillating water column converter, showing air flow on (c) rising and (d) falling waves.

Another type of wave energy converter is the circular 'clam' or 'atoll' device, designed so that waves from any direction are guided by a system of radiating vanes to a central vertical channel where the water spirals downwards to drive a turbine and generator. Such converters would be deployed in arrays rather than in long rows (as in Figure 49a and b), but they are big, and large numbers would be required to generate useful amounts of power commercially. A 60 m diameter 'clam', for example, could generate an average of about 600 kW (with a peak of about 2 MW), so about 1300 of them would be required to equal the power provided by a 1 GW conventional power station operating at 80% capacity.

Nevertheless, wave energy *has* been successfully harnessed, but on a scale of hundreds of kilowatts to a megawatt or two, rather than the hundreds or thousands of megawatts of conventional power stations. The Japanese, for example, have installed hundreds of small-scale oscillating water column converters (Figure 49b–d), to power buoys and lighthouses, each requiring 70–120 kW, and other countries have done the same. (The Japanese installed a larger scale trial device of this kind in the Sea of Japan in 1987, but it produced considerably less than the predicted peak output of 2 MW.) In Norway and in the Hebrides off north-west Scotland, small installations have been built where steep rocky coasts face deep water, with narrow bays and inlets that 'funnel' landwards. The crest length of incoming waves is progressively decreased and their height correspondingly increased. The wave energy can be used either directly to drive converters that work on principles similar to that illustrated in Figure 49b–d; or indirectly to fill reservoirs behind small dams: the resulting head of water is then used to drive turbines, as in any small hydroelectric plant, and the waves act merely to keep the reservoir filled.

Active interest in developing wave energy systems continues in Japan, Norway and North America, and it is possible that competitive large-scale conversion of wave power into electricity may prove feasible in some locations. In the UK, wave energy research has had little government support since the 1980s, but continues with funding from private industry, and there are plans for a major project to be based at Dounreay, formerly the site of Britain's prototype fast breeder reactor (Section 2.1.2).

4.6 Summary of Section 4

Table 6 summarizes the *total global* energy output from 'alternative' energy sources including geothermal for completeness. It is crucial to bear in mind that only a small to very small fraction of these totals can ever be tapped for our needs, which amount to about 3.5×10^{20} J y^{-1} (or 3.9×10^{20} J y^{-1} if we include subsistence biomass use), equivalent to about 10^{13} W continuous power.

Table 6 Total annual energy produced globally by 'alternative' energy sources

Energy source	Annual energy output (approx.)	
	J y^{-1}	W
geothermal	3×10^{20}	10^{13}
solar	3×10^{24}	10^{17}
biomass	10^{22}	10^{14}
wind	3×10^{23}	10^{16}
waves	3×10^{22} (10% of wind)	10^{15}
falling water	3×10^{20}	10^{13}
tidal	8×10^{19}	10^{12}

1 Surface energy resources include those derived by exploitation of solar radiation either directly, or indirectly through biomass, wind, hydroelectric and wave sources. The last two depend also on the Earth's gravitational forces. Tidal power depends only on gravitational interaction with the Sun and the Moon.

2 Of the above energy sources, only hydropower was making a significant contribution to global or UK energy supply in the early 1990s, but most of them have considerable potential for power generation at economic rates; wind power in particular has shown rapid development in some regions (as has geothermal power generation; Section 3).

3   Large-scale conversion of solar energy to electricity, whether by means of focusing collectors (heliostats) or by photovoltaic cells, is not likely to be an economic proposition in the foreseeable future. However, the increasing small-scale use of flat-plate solar collectors for water and space heating, and of photovoltaic solar cells to generate electricity for individual buildings and local communities, can raise living standards in developing countries and could significantly reduce dependence on fossil fuels and nuclear power. The biomass energy potential is vast and, with appropriate investment and lead time, growing biomass energy crops to produce storable and transportable fuels could replace much of the demand for conventional energy resources. In industrialized countries there is increasing focus on incineration of biomass and on extracting 'biofuels' (especially biogas) from organic refuse.

4   Although the power produced by wind turbines varies as the cube of the wind speed, wind is a relatively 'dilute' energy source, because air has a low density. The largest wind generators can produce up to about 3 MW of electrical power, and are competitive with electricity from conventional sources, but large wind farms are needed to generate electricity on any significant scale.

5   The power output of hydroelectric schemes depends on the working head and the discharge rate; therefore, such schemes are developed ideally in mountainous regions (large head) or through estuarial barrages (exploiting large tidal discharges). The large-scale hydropower potential of mountainous regions in the UK and a number of other European countries has already been realized (about 5×10^{16} J y^{-1}), but the potential for small-scale use of hydroelectricity is enormous.

6   The Severn estuary is one of the few ideal sites on a global scale for developing tidal power, with a peak output potential exceeding 7000 MW (22×10^{16} J y^{-1}). However, the huge investment and long lead times of tidal barrage schemes has prevented large-scale use of tidal energy.

7   Harnessing wave energy is more difficult technically than tidal or hydropower conversion, requiring complex converters. Because wave energy is a 'dilute' energy source, large arrays of converters would be required for significant levels of power generation.

Small-scale use of surface energy resources

A highly practical demonstration of a self-sufficient rural community functioning independently of conventional energy sources is the Centre for Alternative Technology at Machynlleth, Powys, mid-Wales. Here, hydropower, wind power, biomass, active and passive solar heating and photovoltaics, as well as energy conservation, are combined to maintain an environment-friendly lifestyle.

Question 19

The basic equation for photosynthesis reads:

$$6CO_2 + 6H_2O + 2.8 \times 10^6 \text{ J} \rightarrow C_6H_{12}O_6 + 6O_2$$

i.e. 2.8×10^6 J of energy are required to form a mole of carbohydrate, and this energy is released as heat when the carbohydrate is consumed or burnt. How does the calorific value of unprocessed biomass compare with that of bituminous coal (about 30 MJ kg^{-1})? (Relative atomic masses are C = 12, H = 1, O = 16). (See Box on moles in Section 2.1.1.)

Question 20

Decide, giving reasons, whether each of the following statements about alternative energy resources is true or false.

A   The char produced by pyrolysis of organic material has a calorific value no higher than that of raw biomass.

B   For the same wind speed in each location, a wind turbine sited on top of a hill will yield more power than one sited in shallow coastal waters.

C   Pumped storage schemes provide one answer to the problem of using unpredictable renewable energy resources (e.g. wind and wave energies) at times of peak demand.

D   Whereas the turbines used to exploit tidal power may be single or double direction generators, those used in oscillating water column converters are only double direction generators.

This is a good time to view Video Band 13.

Video Band 13   Renewable Energies

Speakers

John Wright	The Open University
Geoff Brown	The Open University
Dick Beniot	Oxbow Geothermal Corporation
Jim Anderson	Mammoth Pacific L.P.
Dave Rib	KJC Operating Company
Tim Smith	Woodland Biomass Power Ltd.
Paul Gipe	American Wind Energy Association

This programme was made in 1992–93.

The programme touches briefly on nuclear power, represented by Wylfa power station in Anglesey (Plate 41), the last of the Magnox stations to be commissioned (1971), rated at 840 MW and supplying base load power (see Figure 56). It then focuses on the following renewable energy technologies: geothermal, solar-thermal, photovoltaics, biomass, wind. After watching the programme you should be able to answer Questions 21 to 25.

Question 21

(a) Which component of Figure 29 is represented by the Dixie Valley geothermal plant in Nevada, and which by the Mammoth Lakes plant in southern California?

(b) How do depths of aquifers and temperatures of geothermal fluid compare at Dixie Valley and Mammoth Lakes?

(c) Electricity from Dixie Valley costs about 8 cents per kWh, twice as much as the average for California geothermal electricity. What is the reason for the difference?

(d) The same volumes of geothermal fluid are used at both Dixie Valley and Mammoth Lakes, yet one generates twice as much electricity as the other. Why?

(e) What is the principal reason why scaling of pipes occurs at Dixie Valley?

(f) Seasonal and diurnal temperature variations affect efficiency at Mammoth Lakes much more than at Dixie Valley. Why is this, and what legal environmental constraint at Mammoth Lakes further affects efficiency?

Question 22

(a) Is the cost of electricity generated at the solar-thermal plant in California's Mojave Desert (Plate 48) greater or less than geothermal electricity?

(b) Why was output at this plant less than average during 1991–92?

(c) What happens at this plant when power is needed on cloudy days or at night?

(d) What is the big advantage of photovoltaic technology as portrayed in the programme, and what property of photovoltaic electricity presents an additional difficulty in large-scale power generation using this technology?

Question 23

(a) In terms of energy density, fossil fuels are superior to biomass burning. True or false, and why?

(b) Biomass burning has a major advantage over fossil fuels in the context of global warming. What is it?

(c) How can biomass be used to make liquid or gaseous fuels?

Question 24

(a) How valid is the claim that the large areas of land taken up by wind farms are not necessarily 'sterilized' for any other use?

(b) The wind farm on Anglesey, shown in the video, consists of 24 turbines rated at 300 kW each (i.e. 7.2 MW total). How many such turbines would be needed to replace the rated 840 MW of Wylfa?

Question 25

(a) Renewable energies are widely held to be clean and sustainable technologies. Consider each of the technologies reviewed in the video and comment on the validity of this claim.

(b) What is the principal reason why it would be extremely difficult, if not actually impossible, to generate our present-day electricity requirements entirely from renewable energy sources?

5 FUTURE ENERGY DEMAND AND SUPPLY

In the UK we are fortunate in having large enough coal reserves to produce most of our electrical power — an important factor that has delayed the need to expand rapidly the generation of power from nuclear or renewable resources.

S238 The Earth's Physical Resources, *Block 5, Part 1 (1983)*

So far as human society is concerned, the only certain thing about the future is that nothing is certain. To take a small and parochial but telling example, few in Britain could have foreseen the day in October 1992 when the Government announced the proposed immediate closure of 31 coal mines out of a total of 50 still working at the time. At a stroke, the value of huge tonnages of proved reserves of what had for centuries been considered Britain's principal long-term foundation for energy self-sufficiency, namely coal, was reduced from around £35 per tonne to £0 per tonne. As outlined in Block 4 *Energy 1*, the object of the closures was purely commercial: to cut costs to the recently privatized electricity generating companies and hence to the consumers. This was to be achieved by bringing in cheap coal from abroad and by replacing older coal-fired power stations by gas-fired plant fuelled with North Sea gas (the 'dash for gas'). The eventual aim was to make the British coal industry smaller and more efficient and attractive for privatization. Meantime, the Government was still paying its subsidy of £1.2 billions annually to the nuclear industry (the 'nuclear levy', Section 2.1.4) to keep the cost of nuclear electricity competitive with that from other fuels. It also continued to import nuclear-generated electricity from France, equivalent to 5 million tonnes of coal per year. As discussed in Block 4 *Energy 1*, coal had historically been Britain's most abundant energy resource, and mining had for centuries been a traditional occupation in many parts of the country, where pits formed a strong social focus for local communities.

The pit closures: causes and consequences (social and environmental)

There was a vociferous and widespread public outcry at the announcement of the coal mine closures, not least because of the social implications of large-scale unemployment among long-established mining communities (estimates put the total who would be made jobless virtually overnight at 50 000–100 000 — not only the miners themselves, but people in support and service industries too). Many people also felt that there were political overtones, recalling the many bitter confrontations between Government and unions during the year-long miners' strike of 1984–85.

The pit closures had nothing to do with environmental concerns. The proposals did not mention the UK commitment at the Earth Summit in Rio de Janeiro a couple of months earlier, to stabilize (if not reduce) emissions of the main greenhouse gas, carbon dioxide, by reducing the use of fossil fuels. This is a puzzling omission, for it could have been cogently argued that

in the long run the virtual demise of Britain's deep-mined coal industry is a desirable outcome. Underground coal mining is difficult, uncomfortable and dangerous, it produces unsightly waste tips that must be landscaped, and it causes surface subsidence. Coal is a 'dirty' fuel, emitting nearly twice as much CO_2 and significantly more SO_2 per unit of energy than does natural gas (Figure 30), and thus contributes more to global warming and acid rain (though it must be acknowledged that technological improvements — especially fluidized bed combustion and flue gas desulphurization — can mitigate the environmental impacts of burning coal). The decision to close the pits had nothing to do with geology either, except in so far as British coal occurs in seams that are a metre or two thick, lie hundreds of metres below ground, and are costly to extract, whereas the cheap imports come from seams that are more than ten metres thick and less than a hundred metres deep, which is why they are cheap to extract.

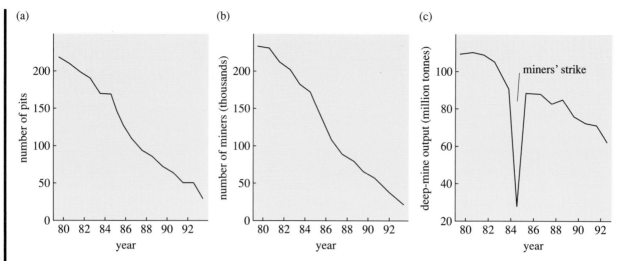

Figure 50 The decline in UK deep-mined coal from 1980 to 1993, as shown by three indicators: (a) number of deep mines (pits); (b) number of miners employed; (c) output from deep mines.

In fact, the writing had been on the wall for Britain's deep-mined coal industry since before the miners' strike. After the strike, moves towards privatization of the coal industry and away from reliance on coal as the UK's principal energy source began to gather momentum. The decline is graphically illustrated in Figure 50 and is consistent with the 1991 Rothschild report for the Government, which suggested that a privatized coal industry would consist of no more than 12 deep mines.

Moreover, in 1993 the privatized electricity companies (PowerGen and National Power) negotiated contracts with British Coal that reduced the amount of UK coal supplied to them from 40 million tonnes in 1992–93 (compared with 65 million tonnes in 1991–92), down to 30 million tonnes in each of the next four years — and 10–12 million tonnes of that would continue to be provided by opencast operations, which had been producing around 15 million tonnes annually through the 1980s and into the early 1990s.

The coal industry's problems were compounded by the following factors.

(a) The nuclear industry managed to improve efficiency and increase its share of the electricity market in 1993–94 to more than 25%.

(b) Stockpiles of coal at power stations already stood at 40 million tonnes and were growing by 1 million tonnes a month.

(c) More gas-fired power stations were planned and approved (though it was claimed by some authorities that they were more expensive than coal-fired ones).

(d) The Government agreed to allow increased burning in power stations of the oil-based fuel *orimulsion*, a bitumen–water mixture imported from Venezuela and said by environmentalists to be the 'dirtiest fuel in the world', by industrialists

to be 'as clean as any other fuel'. Against this background of a shrinking market, the harder the miners worked to improve efficiency and productivity in order to produce more coal more cheaply, the more likely they were to find themselves out of a job.

Although the public outcry that followed announcement of the pit closures did lead to government undertakings to review the situation, the stark facts remained: in the absence of any sizeable market for deep-mined British coal, more mines would close sooner or later.

An environmental consequence of the accelerated pit closure programme, not anticipated by politicians and economists, has been pollution of rivers by large volumes of acid (pH 3 to 5) and metal-rich water emerging at the surface from closed mines, which quickly became flooded by groundwater as soon as the pumps were switched off — which is why the mines cannot thereafter be reopened. Networks of underground workings greatly enhance the secondary permeability of rocks and they literally channel water into underground 'rivers', which can have high rates of discharge when they reach the surface. The waters are acid and metal rich because for centuries mining has exposed sulphide minerals (especially the iron sulphide pyrite, FeS_2) in the coal to the air in the workings. Oxidation of sulphide to sulphate produces sulphuric acid which dissolves the iron and other metals. Well-documented studies in South Wales and north-east England have shown that when these waters reach the rivers they kill fish and other organisms, and effectively sterilize the stream bed with deposits of iron oxide. The research suggests that it would be cheaper to spend a few million pounds sterling to keep the pumps running in abandoned mines and thus prevent pollution occurring, than to spend many more million pounds on cleaning up the pollution after it has occurred. In the mid-1990s, the more expensive cure was being preferred to the less costly prevention.

The following extract from an *Observer* article in April 1993 represents a typical comment on the pit closure policy.

> … what stands out more than anything else in the Government's plans is the complete absence of any clear, coherent vision of how the country's energy resources and reserves should be marshalled for the long-term. No other country in the world with such an attractive variety of energy sources at its disposal — coal, oil, gas, nuclear and alternative options — would throw such an opportunity to the wolves of the free market.

The words 'free market' in that extract go some way to explaining what seems to be an inconsistency at the heart of the pit closure policy: on the one hand, money must be sent abroad to pay for the imported coal, while on the other, tens of thousands of redundant miners and ancillary workers must be paid unemployment and other benefits.

 Would it not make more sense to use British coal and thus keep the money in the country, and at the same time receive tax revenues from working miners instead of handing out unemployment pay?

 In the context of the international free market, such questions are naive. Companies in the private sector are free to deploy financial resources in any way they wish, to maximize profits, which can feed back into the system through taxation, and indirectly contribute to supporting the unemployed.

In the event, the free market may turn out to have benefited some mining communities more than would have been predicted in October 1992. During 1994 some half dozen pits were reopened under private sector management (some with investment from overseas) to supply domestic and industrial markets, which require coal of higher quality (and at higher prices) than that used for electricity generation. The rest of the British coal industry — including the 16 or so public sector pits still working under British Coal management — was 'packaged' for privatization into three main regions and sold off at the end of 1994, yielding some £800 million to the Government. About 25 deep mines were in production early in 1995, 21 of them under the ownership of RJB Mining.

For comparison, it is worth noting that the much smaller French and Belgian deep-mined coal industries had previously been all but closed down, but that governments of other European countries (Germany and Spain, for example) continued to subsidize their coal industries, even to the extent of financing development of new pits.

The abrupt closure of most of Britain's remaining deep-mined coal industry provides another good example of how resource planning and policy depends more upon a combination of economic relationships between demand, supply and price on the one hand, and political considerations on the other, than upon geological availability (see Activity 1 and Question 6, also Block 4 *Energy 1*). It is also a powerful illustration of how difficult it must be to plan ahead, when lead times are on a scale of years to decades, while the timescale of political and economic change is commonly weeks or months (or less). The problems are most crucial for the energy industries, because without energy nothing functions.

5.1 Energy forecasting

Any attempt to forecast energy demand must recognize that the projection for each type of fuel or energy source is related to the question of what *form* future energy requirements will take, and the latter will be dependent on economic factors and political decisions, as we have seen. This raises several important questions. For example, what proportion of fossil fuels will go to produce electricity, in which about 70% of the energy production potential is lost in power stations that are only 30% efficient? What proportion will go to driving cars, trains, aircraft, ships and so on? If oil is to be used as a fuel, for how long can it continue to supply the petrochemicals industry? Can we actually locate and extract the necessary reserves in the amounts required? To what extent can we reduce our dependence on fossil fuels? Can other sources of power expand to reduce that dependence, especially as concern about global warming and acid rain grows year by year? These are just some of the questions you should bear in mind as you read on.

One way of trying to visualize how energy resources might be used to maximum advantage is by the construction of 'scenarios', or imagined pictures of the future, which attempt to incorporate all known factors of importance. There are three main types of scenario:

1 *Historical growth scenarios* assume that energy consumption will continue to rise along the same path as it has done historically.

2 *Technological fix scenarios* reflect efforts to reduce demands for energy through the application of energy-saving techniques leading to lower growth rates, or the introduction of new, more economic methods of producing and using energy in order to sustain growth.

3 *Zero growth scenarios* imply that society would make the voluntary or enforced decision that it had reached the end of growth.

These scenarios are not mutually exclusive because policy-makers in different nations and national groups have radically different views of energy futures.

Figure 51 exemplifies the historical growth scenario. From the mid-1950s, and especially during the 1960s, oil became increasingly plentiful and cheap; partly as a consequence, global energy production rose at something like 4.5% annually (a doubling time of about 15 years). The forecast embodied in Figure 51 reflects the view of many people at the time: they saw no reason why this growth should not continue.

⬤ What happened to prevent this growth from continuing?

◯ The Middle East oil producers—then as now the world's principal source of supply—felt that the price of their chief asset was too low and the resource was being squandered. So they took action.

Oil prices quadrupled during 1973–74. With hindsight it is easy to say that the rest of the world (especially the industrialized part of it) should have seen this coming. In fact, the 'Club of Rome' (a group of eminent scientists and other professionals), in their publications *Blueprint for Survival* and *Limits to Growth* which appeared in 1972, warned that the exploitation of most resources, not just energy, was increasing exponentially and that such a policy was (and remains) environmentally unsustainable. Few paid them any heed, however, and in the event, it was economic not environmental factors that forced a zero-growth scenario upon the world for a couple of years in the mid-1970s. This can be seen in Figure 52 which summarizes global energy production up to 1992.

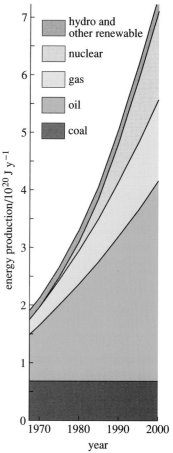

Figure 51 Projections of future global energy production, including possible contributions from different energy sources. Based on 4.5% annual growth rate overall, published in 1971. (See also note in Figure 52 caption.)

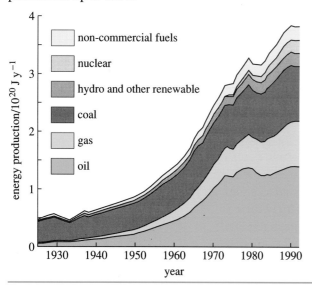

Figure 52 Actual global energy production from 1925 to 1992. 'Non-commercial fuels' refers to subsistence burning of biomass; see Section 4.1.3. This is another kind of stacked area diagram (compare Figures 19, 20 and 51); for example, the energy produced by coal in 1991–92 was $3.0 - 2.1 \times 10^{20}$ J $= 0.9 \times 10^{20}$ J.

● What sort of scenario(s) is/are depicted in Figure 52?

○ In Figure 52, the historical growth scenario of Figure 51 ends abruptly in the early 1970s, to be replaced by essentially an alternation of zero-growth and technological-fix scenarios. The zero-growth 'dips' of the early 1970s, 1980s and 1990s are separated by quite steep upward curves, but the gradients do not steepen with time as in Figure 51.

The two graphs in Figures 51 and 52 show some interesting features. For example:

1   The 1971 projection assumed that neither coal nor 'alternatives' would increase its share of overall energy production at all, presumably because of the prevailing cheapness of oil.

2   The 1971 projection assumed also that the nuclear contribution to global energy production would greatly increase. Although nuclear power stations were being commissioned from the mid-1950s onwards, and proliferated during the 1960s (Section 2), their contribution was not globally significant until the start of the 1970s; at that time the many problems that have beset the industry were less obvious and nuclear power was still regarded as a cheap form of energy.

3   Coal was the dominant energy source until the 1950s, and it is worth emphasizing that use of natural gas did not become widespread until oil production began to increase — before that, most of the gas used came from distilling coal. In the UK, and probably elsewhere too, the local gas plant producing tar and coke as by-products was a familiar feature of urban landscapes until well into the 1960s.

Question 26

Compare Figures 51 and 52. What differences do you observe in the 1990 figures for:

(a) total global energy production;

(b) the relative contributions of fossil fuels to the total;

(c) the nuclear share of the total;

(d) the alternatives share of the total?

It is worth recalling also that the Shah of Iran was overthrown and replaced by Ayatollah Khomeini in 1979–80. Soon after that the Iran–Iraq war began, and the price of oil reached an all-time high of nearly 40 dollars a barrel. The net result was that total global commercial energy output in 1982 (Figure 52) was actually *less* than in 1979 (about 2.8×10^{20} J, compared with 2.9×10^{20} J).

As we read in Block 4 *Energy 1*, the oil price rises of the early 1970s and 1980s encouraged oil companies to look for oil elsewhere than the Middle East, and the oil fields of Alaska, the North Sea, the Niger Delta and the Gulf of Mexico became major producers. In addition, there was a move towards energy efficiency and conservation in the use of fossil fuels, so that less oil was actually needed. So successful were these actions in reducing demand that the oil price fell sharply in 1986 to about 15 dollars a barrel. Not only had the world come to rely somewhat less on Middle East oil, but the incentive to develop the alternative renewable energy sources also became less strong.

Political factors affecting supply and demand (and hence price) in the petroleum industry exerted a major influence on global economies for over two decades — and may well continue to do so. Figure 53 shows how the oil price fluctuated through more than two decades from 1970. There is a degree of symmetry about Figure 53: the price of crude oil in 1993–94 was back to its 1970 (adjusted) level of around 15 dollars a barrel. However, the large short-term fluctuations of the intervening years show how hard it must be to make reliable forward projections.

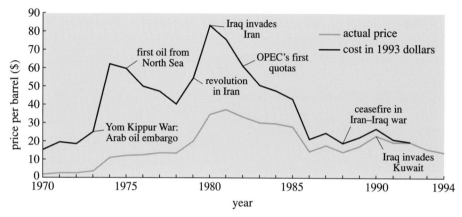

Figure 53 Changes in the price of crude oil (US dollars per barrel) from 1970 to 1993, showing how major world events influenced the fluctuations. Note the overall symmetry and the considerable price inflation from the mid-1970s to the mid-1980s. Note: Details on this graph may differ from those on other graphs of oil price changes with time. That is because different authorities use different methods for calculating annual price averages.

5.1.1 Forecasting energy demand in the UK

Figures 51 to 53 and Question 26 point out the perils of prediction quite well. But in some respects it could be easier to compile 'global' graphs like those in Figures 51 and 52 than to forecast the use of energy (or of any other major resource) for an individual country.

○ Why is such forecasting difficult, and why is it necessary in the first place?

○ It is difficult because of the problem of lead times: any new development (building a power station or factory, developing a mine, quarry or oil field) can take 5–10 years (or more in some cases) and requires investment with a guaranteed return at the end. If demand for the commodity in question has fallen in the intervening period, there will be little or no return on the investment. The other side of the coin is that forecasting is necessary precisely because of those 5–10 year lead times. It is no good suddenly realizing that demand for (say) electricity has gone up by 25% in five years, and that the power supply industry cannot cope because no new power stations were commissioned.

By way of illustrative example, let us examine part of the UK electricity-generating industry's record in forecasting, in an historical context. Figure 54 compares the electricity actually used between 1956 and 1980 with two estimates of the demand made by the electricity supply industry. The *estimates* were very similar, and both differ by the same substantial margin from the amount actually used.

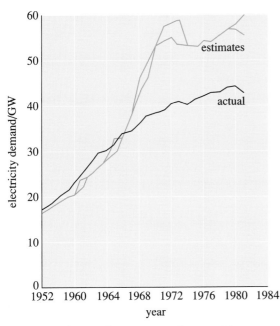

Figure 54 Two estimates of the demand for electricity in Britain compared with the actual demand from 1956 to 1980.

It is clear that as the economy boomed between the mid-1950s and the mid-1960s, demand slightly exceeded estimates. Thereafter, however, estimates of demand exceeded the quantity of power actually used, particularly during the recession of the middle to late 1970s. To have criticized what was then the Central Electricity Generating Board (CEGB) for the later overcapacity would be to criticize it for failure to foresee the recession. As the recession was brought on in large part by reactions to the Arab–Israeli war of 1973, criticism of subsequent overcapacity is equivalent to criticism of failure to anticipate a particular episode in Middle East history. The estimates of demand for the 1970s had, of course, to be made during the 1960s. To condemn the CEGB planners for failing to foresee the Arab–Israeli war of 1973 and its consequences, when during the boom years of the 1960s they were estimating demand for the 1970s, is plainly ridiculous.

Figure 55 illustrates another important point. It shows the CEGB's actual surplus capacity (as opposed to the excess of estimated over actual demand shown in Figure 54) from 1963 to 1981. The story is broadly the same: there was apparently a particularly large overcapacity during the mid-1970s. In interpreting Figure 55, however, it is necessary to bear in mind that some surplus capacity must be built into the system as a contingency against breakdowns. Moreover, as power stations get bigger the reserve requirement must be increased, for any single breakdown means a greater proportional loss of capacity.

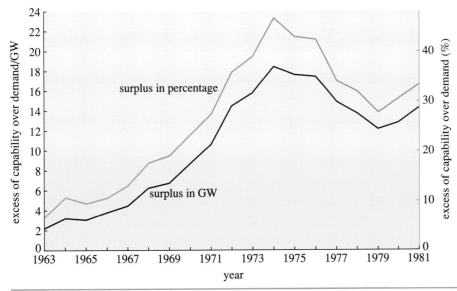

Figure 55 The CEGB's surplus generating capacity from 1963 to 1980 in GW (lower curve, left-hand scale) and as a percentage of the actual demand (upper curve, right-hand scale).

To emphasize the point, look back to Figure 42 and estimate the extent of fluctuation in electricity demand during a day.

Demand fluctuates by a factor of between about 1.5 and 2 during the day, depending on time of year (and it can fluctuate by a factor of up to 3 during any one year).

So it is not surprising that extra capacity has to be built into the generating system, and Figure 56 shows how a hierarchy of generating plant is used in the UK for different periods of time, to cope with fluctuations in demand; it illustrates that it is convenient to have a 'mix' of energy sources.

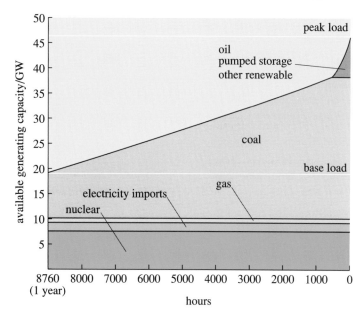

Figure 56 The amount and duration (hours) of use of different types of generating plant in the UK in the early 1990s, and the order in which they were used as the power demand rose. The base load is the minimum continuous demand.

As noted in Section 4.3, nuclear plants are not easily closed down over short periods, so they carry much of the base load. Figure 56 represents a fair picture of the UK situation in the early 1990s, though the move to replace coal with gas for power generation, and a more widespread use of renewables, especially wind energy (Section 4.2), has shifted the balance somewhat. But the basic principles remain the same: additional plant is needed to cope not only with normal fluctuations in demand, but also with additional loads caused by, say, a prolonged cold spell, with breakdowns, or with interruptions in supply of one or other fuel (e.g. oil in the mid-1970s, coal in 1984).

Energy conservation

Most conservation measures are aimed at reducing the amount of energy needed for a particular task. Home insulation and improved boiler designs are obvious examples of ways in which heat energy can be saved; more efficient electrical appliances means less electricity is used; whilst conservation in the transport area can arise from the wider use of public transport, car pooling, improved maintenance of vehicle engines, reduced speed limits, and cycling or walking rather than driving. It is well known that heat losses from a typical house can be cut by almost an order of magnitude by incorporating cavity wall insulation, fibreglass loft insulation and double glazing. The statutory insulation requirements for new buildings were doubled in the UK as long ago as 1975, but they still remain well below those obtaining in countries such as Denmark.

Another way of conserving energy is to improve the efficiency of the heat source, and this brings us back to the low efficiency of electricity generating turbines. In order to extract the maximum generating capacity from steam turbines, the lowest practical exit temperature has to be achieved, resulting in vast volumes of cooling water at about 30 °C, too cool for any use apart from heating greenhouses. Overall thermal efficiency can be improved, however, by designing power stations to produce both electricity and usable heat; these are known as *combined heat and power (CHP) stations* (Figure 57). In such stations a small part of the generating efficiency is sacrificed so that hot water, and in some designs steam, can be drawn off at usefully high temperatures for industrial, horticultural or local domestic heating schemes of the type described for semi-thermal geothermal resources in Section 3.2. In this way, the overall efficiency of CHP schemes can exceed 70%.

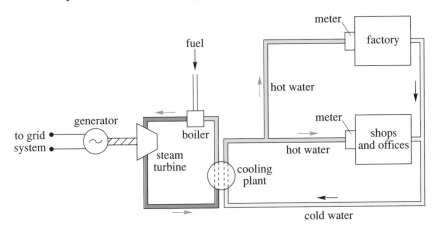

Figure 57 A combined heat and power station showing heat loads and power output.

Of course, there are some difficulties: for example, power stations need to be smaller than those built hitherto, which produce far more excess heat than can be used locally. Moreover, CHP schemes need to be sited in urban locations with high levels of population, so that there is a demand for both heat and electricity. Although CHP schemes have not yet become widely developed in Britain, 15% of industrial electricity requirements are met by such systems, usually where power generation is linked to heat produced by industrial processes, as in parts of the paper and chemicals industries.

However, this amounts only to 2–3% of national electricity production, compared with 10% in Germany and about 30% in Holland — but the proportion is growing. For example, a 30 MW gas-fired CHP plant was commissioned in 1993 on the site of London's former Smithfield market, to supply electricity and district heating to much of the capital's commercial centre, the East End. It is claimed that conversion efficiencies are as high as 90%, that the City's emissions of CO_2 have been halved, and those of sulphur and nitrogen oxides reduced to a minimum (other than those emanating from the exhausts of motor vehicles still clogging the City's streets).

A short case study

We have touched briefly on some of the factors that can influence energy forecasting, and the perils of prediction mentioned earlier are if anything more starkly illustrated in Table 7 than in Figures 51 and 52. The table shows examples of two contrasted scenarios applied to energy demand in UK and, by implication, in other industrialized nations. They were compiled in 1979, i.e. after the oil price crisis of the mid-1970s and before the miners' strike of 1984–85. You can compare the forecasts with the actual picture of energy demand and use in 1990, also given in Table 7. The two scenarios are summarized below:

A combined historical growth/technological fix scenario using projections from 1976 data was developed by the UK Department of Energy and was based on two main assumptions: (a) that energy consumption, and national industrial and commercial output, as measured by the *Gross Domestic Product* (GDP), would grow smoothly at a moderate rate, 2.5% per annum; (b) that overall energy demand would evolve smoothly with rising energy prices and with a tendency for domestic consumption to level off with some conservation measures.

A combined technological fix/low growth scenario was proposed by the IIED (International Institute for Environment and Development) and assumed: (a) the UK could move into a prosperous low-energy future with no more than moderate changes so long as the proven technical advances in energy use and conservation were applied rigorously; (b) industrial fuel consumption per pound sterling of turnover would fall by some 22% owing to energy savings using existing conservation techniques; (c) insulation and thermally efficient equipment would produce energy savings of around 50% in domestic and commercial premises.

Table 7 Comparisons between Department of Energy and IIED low-growth scenarios for energy futures in the UK, compiled in 1979, with actual data for 1976 and 1990

	1976 data	Dept of Energy scenario		IIED scenario		1990 data
		2000	2025	2000	2025	
Fuel consumption/mtce y$^{-1\dagger}$						
coal	124	155	203	116	128	85
oil	150	165	145	130	82	155
natural gas	41	76	9	51	37	110
nuclear	9	72	239	27	22	15
renewables	2	2	9	6	26	3
totals/mtce y$^{-1\dagger}$	326	470	605	330	295	368
percentage of 1976 totals	100	144	186	101	91	113
totals/10^{18} J y^{-1}	9.3	13.4	17.2	9.4	8.4	10.4
Electricity production*/(10^{18} J y^{-1})	0.79	1.30	2.05	0.76	0.76	1.08

†We have quoted fuel consumption in million tonnes coal equivalent per year for ready comparison with data that commonly appear in the national press; 35 mtce y^{-1} is equivalent to about 10^{18} J y^{-1}.

* These figures need to be multiplied by a factor of between 3 and 4 to give the quantity of energy consumed in the production of electricity.

Question 27

(a) What are the principal differences between the two scenarios?

(b) In what major respects did neither of the two scenarios get it right, according to the 1990 data?

Another factor that may have occurred to you when studying Table 7 and answering Question 27 is that energy conservation measures (including improved energy efficiency of turbines, engines and so on) probably contributed to the relatively small increase in total energy consumption between 1976 and 1990. This represents a closer approach to the IIED than to the Department of Energy scenario.

5.1.2 *Availability and characteristics of different energy sources*

It is easier to criticize energy policies and forecasts (or even the lack of any) than it is to formulate them. Before even beginning to speculate on what might lie ahead for the UK energy scene, it may be useful to review the principal characteristics of the 'basket' of energy resources available.

Fossil fuels are the principal traditional energy source, but on combustion they all emit CO_2 and varying amounts of SO_2, along with nitrogen oxides. Every atom of fossil fuel carbon burned adds a molecule of CO_2 to the atmospheric burden of this gas and may contribute to global warming. SO_2 and nitrogen oxides are responsible for acid rain.

Coal is the most abundant of the fossil fuels but has the lowest 'energy density' and the greatest pollution potential. Commercial coal contains 5–10% or more of non-combustible mineral impurity (ash), around 1% of sulphur, and other elements in trace amounts, such as chlorine, uranium (Section 2.2.1) and arsenic. So-called clean coal technologies have been developed to improve combustion efficiency and reduce pollution. They include fluidized bed combustion with flue-gas desulphurization, which involves adding crushed limestone to the coal to remove the sulphur as gypsum ($CaSO_4.2H_2O$), as well as dust extraction to trap fine ash and some of the trace elements. As we saw at the start of Section 5, however, there was a move away from coal by the UK Government during the late 1980s and early 1990s, despite the fact that coal remains Britain's most abundant energy raw material. On a global scale coal provides over 40% of total electrical energy production, and there is enough coal to sustain demand at present levels for a couple of centuries, even without any new reserves being found.

Oil is a more versatile fuel than coal and has higher 'energy density', not least because of its low to zero ash content, but it still produces sulphur and nitrogen oxide emissions as well as CO_2 (though less than coal per unit of energy obtained; see Figure 30). Unburnt hydrocarbons and carbon monoxide from motor vehicle exhausts can cause high levels of pollution in urban regions (unless the vehicles are fitted with catalytic exhaust systems which virtually eliminate such pollutants). Global oil reserves are sufficient for several decades at 1990s consumption levels. Major new reserves will be increasingly difficult and costly to extract, however, and it may be difficult for oil to continue providing a third of the world's energy needs (see Figure 52).

Gas has the highest 'energy density' of all three fossil fuels and is widely held to be a 'clean' fuel, because it leaves no ash and contains virtually no sulphur; but burning gas still produces nitrogen oxides as well as CO_2 (though less than or oil per unit of energy obtained; Figure 30). Reserves of natural gas are also sufficient for several decades at 1990s' levels of demand.

Nuclear fission is by far the most concentrated energy source available, and the actual *generation* of nuclear power releases no CO_2, SO_2, nitrogen oxides or other chemicals. However, radioactive by-products can contaminate air, water and soil over wide areas, unless very strictly controlled (which all too often is not done), and the radioactivity can last for centuries to millennia. The nuclear industry faces an uncertain future, although known reserves of uranium are sufficient to last the lifetime of reactors so far constructed.

'Alternative' energy sources are all 'clean' as well as renewable, the 'fuel' costs nothing and contributes neither to global warming nor to acid rain. But they have other drawbacks, chiefly because of their low 'energy density', which means that very large areas of land are needed for significant levels of power generation, at least from the *surface* sources of alternative energy, and in the main they are not transportable, so power stations must be built near to the energy source. Nevertheless, their combined potential is considerable: for example, it has been estimated that the UK could provide nearly half its electrical power requirements from alternative sources, especially if energy conservation policies were to be implemented.

5.1.3 Relative costs of different energy sources

This issue is somewhat analogous to questions like: how long is a piece of string? It all depends on how we do the sums. Thus, in 1994 the price of a unit (1 kWh) of electricity to domestic consumers in the UK was close to 8 pence (i.e. £0.08p kWh^{-1}). For comparison, the cost per equivalent unit of domestic gas was about 1.5p and that of an equivalent unit of motor fuel was about 4–5p kWh^{-1} (depending on type of fuel and where we bought it).

Clearly then, irrespective of energy source, electricity must be generated at a *cost* sufficiently below the *price* to consumers to cover overheads and loan repayments and to leave a margin of profit. Taking the case of wind energy as an example, Table 8 shows a range of calculated costs per kWh for the early 1990s, assuming a loan payback period of 20 years, a range of initial investment costs and average annual wind speeds, and different rates of interest on the loan repayment.

Table 8 Estimated costs of wind-generated electricity for the early 1990s, based on a survey of wind energy in Europe (1991)

Installed cost (£ m^{-2} of swept area)*	Mean annual wind speed/m s^{-1}	Cost per unit (pence kWh^{-1}) according to rate of return on loan			
		5%	8%	10%	15%
420	6.5	4.3	5.2	5.8	7.6
350	7.5	3.5	4.2	4.7	6.2
280	8.5	2.4	2.9	3.2	4.2

* This range of costs is approximately equivalent to £600–£1000 per kW of output.

Question 28

What would happen to the costs per kilowatt hour in Table 8,

(a) if the loan period were increased to 25 years,

(b) if the initial capital costs at a site with high average wind speed rose from say, £280 to £350 per m² of swept area? (Qualitative answers only are required).

Calculations of the same general type can be made for any other energy source, and for non-renewables the additional variable of future fuel costs must be built into the estimates. Nor can political and social factors be ignored. For example, the comparative costs of nuclear and coal in Table 9 are at variance with the UK energy picture of the mid-1990s, when nuclear was increasing its share of the market while coal was showing an almost catastrophic decline (Figure 50). This can be attributed in large measure to the fact that the UK Government was subsidizing the nuclear power industry (£1.2 billion annually, Section 2.1.4 and Section 5) but not the coal industry.

Table 9 Estimated comparative costs per unit of electricity from different energy sources for the early 1990s, based on a survey of wind energy in Europe (1991)

Type of energy source	Cost per unit (pence kWh^{-1})
nuclear	6.0–10
gas turbine	2.0–2.9
hydropower	2.0–2.8
coal	2.9–3.9
wind turbine	2.9–5.2

So, electricity from coal mined in Britain in effect 'costs' more than nuclear electricity. In addition, as noted in Section 4.2, the Non-Fossil Fuel Obligation virtually guaranteed a market for wind power in the UK which no doubt contributed to the proliferation of wind farms — helped by a public perception of this energy source as generally clean and non-polluting.

Indeed, during 1993, the Government announced that subsidies on alternative technologies for producing electricity would be extended from five to 20 years, thus ensuring that they would remain competitive with conventional fuels. The subsidies cover wind and hydropower, landfill gas, and incineration not only of domestic and commercial wastes, but also of agricultural and forestry wastes, as well as coppicing on 'wood farms' to provide fuel for power stations.

Question 29

The relative proportions of four categories of energy consumption are given in Table 10, for 1976, 1990 and for the two scenarios presented in Table 7. Briefly describe the difference between expectation and likely outcome, and offer some explanations for the differences.

Table 10 Comparison of actual energy consumption, in percentage terms, in 1976 and 1990 with predictions for the year 2000 according to the scenarios in Table 7

	1976 data	Dept of Energy scenario 2000	IIED scenario 2000	1990 data
industry	43	49	50	27
domestic	25	19	18	27
commercial	11	10	8	13
transport	21	22	24	33

To round off your study of this Section, you should attempt Activity 3, which attempts to pull together several aspects of energy resources which we have been considering.

Activity 3

You know from Block 4 *Energy 1* and earlier Sections of this Block that the UK has access to the full range of energy resources — so how should they be deployed to best advantage?

The edited extract below comes from *The Observer* of 14 March 1993. It was written by James Hann, independent chairman of Scottish Nuclear, under the title: *Wanted: A long-term energy strategy,* and argues that market forces alone must not govern Britain's national energy strategy.

'George the Third ought never to have occurred, as the clerihew goes, and the same could be said of the pits closure 'crisis'. But it did; and if it has achieved nothing else, it has thrown into sharp perspective the difficulties inherent in leaving decisions on energy to a market which is incapable of serving our long-term national interests.

There is a real need for a longer-term, more co-ordinated approach to energy production and consumption, using the disciplines of the market but preventing short-term distortions that put at risk the benefits of a comprehensive long-term policy.

A sensible energy framework would allow considered long-term decisions to be taken and permit market forces to co-exist more easily with monopoly (and duopoly in the case of National Power and PowerGen) regulation.

We must also recognize that our energy management responsibilities transcend national boundaries. The issues facing the energy industry are global. Market forces do not make any allowance for some fundamental factors.

Population is one. Forecasters tell us that by the year 2040 the world's population will have increased from 5 billion to 9 billion people.

The result of such population growth will be that energy demand will inevitably increase. It is expected, for instance, that the demand for electricity will be three times greater than it is today. Where will all this electricity come from?

The recent World Energy Congress in Madrid concluded that there were sufficient reserves of oil for more than four decades, sufficient gas for almost six decades and coal for hundreds of years. But we simply cannot increase fossil fuel burning to that extent. If we meet the growing demand over the next two decades by burning more coal and gas, the planet could be running into serious trouble.

Fluidized beds or gasifiers on coal-fired power stations will help beat acid rain but they will not help CO_2 emissions. Until we know about the greenhouse effect it would be folly to double or treble the coal burned to meet increased demand.

Another danger is an unhealthy dependence on imports of coal and gas from politically unstable areas of supply. This will at best create price volatility and uncertainty and affect our balance of payments — at worst it could affect the supply chain directly. We have seen this problem before with oil.

That is why the future energy mix will need to include both nuclear and renewables. It is also vital that the nuclear industry in the UK continues its progress towards real cost competitiveness while maintaining the highest standards of safety.

Without a significant nuclear element in energy supply, it will not be possible for the Government to meet its obligation to reduce CO_2 emissions to 1990 levels by 2000. And in order simply to maintain the 20% proportion of UK electricity supply currently accounted for by nuclear power, given the 10-year lead time for a nuclear station, up to four new PWR stations would need to be ordered over the next five years.

What we need now is a decision to decree what percentage of the electricity generation market each major fuel should ideally have. I believe the figures should be:

- Coal — that is, mainly domestic coal: between 50% and 55%, against the current 65%.

- Gas should be allowed to increase its share to 15%, due to its cost competitiveness and its lesser impact on the environment.

- Nuclear should remain at between 20% and 25%, which would mean simply replacing the older Magnox plants at the end of their useful lives with new advanced and cost competitive designs.

- Renewables, which more focused research could probably increase to about 5% early next century.

Having made this type of decision, a simple mechanism based on financial incentive and disincentive would enable the concept to work. Indeed, market forces could then operate within these bands to ensure the best possible productivity and competitive prices.

It is astonishing to think that the last time a White Paper on fuel policy was published in the UK was in November 1967, before the discovery of North Sea oil. Since then, there has been fundamental change in the energy market and a much greater realization of the impact of energy on the environment.

That is why we really cannot wait any longer for a sensible long-term energy strategy.'

1   What do you think of the policy? Before making up your mind, look at the few questions below, which may help you focus your ideas.

   (b) What does 'long-term' mean in the context of this proposal?

   (c) Are resources and reserves sufficient to meet the requirements of this policy?

   (d) Does the anticipated three-fold increase in electricity requirements apply globally or to the UK only?

   (e) Why does the proposed policy focus on electricity?

   Having cleared up these points, how do you rate the policy?

2   At the same time as the article was written, the UK Government was reducing UK petroleum revenue tax (i.e. Government tax on the proceeds of petroleum sales by oil companies), and removing tax concessions on the costs of exploration and appraisal of new fields in the North Sea. To what extent might the policy and/or your assessment of it be affected by these actions?

3   Energy conservation is not mentioned in the extract. How important is this omission?

5.2   The future world energy scene — prospects and possibilities

In the previous Section we summarized the main characteristics of presently available sources of energy. From that it seems clear that even maintaining energy production at present levels has major environmental implications, whether in terms of pollution and side-effects or simply of land use and raw material requirements.

To maintain energy production at present levels, therefore, we should turn to an abundant cheap fuel with high 'energy density' that is non-polluting. Two possibilities are outlined below. Neither is ideal but both come nearer to being so than any of those presently in use.

5.2.1   Nuclear fusion

The basis of **nuclear fusion** is collision between nuclei of light atoms at very high speeds to produce larger nuclei with a mass greater than the aggregate mass of the small nuclei. The surplus mass is converted to energy according to the Einstein relation, $E = mc^2$ (see Section 2.1.1). Uncontrolled nuclear fusion is the basis of the hydrogen bomb and the source of all solar energy, but can it be harnessed in a controlled way as an energy resource? One of the world's most lavishly funded research projects has been in progress for several decades (especially in the UK and USA), in attempts to do so.

The fusion reactions which have been studied are those of deuterium and tritium (the heavy isotopes of hydrogen, containing respectively two and three neutrons plus a proton) which fuse to produce either helium-3 or helium-4. For example:

$$\,^{2}_{1}H + \,^{2}_{1}H \rightarrow \,^{3}_{2}He + \,^{1}_{0}n + 5.4 \times 10^{-13} \, J \qquad (5.1)$$
deuterium helium

or

$$\,^{2}_{1}H + \,^{3}_{1}H \rightarrow \,^{4}_{2}He + \,^{1}_{0}n + 3.0 \times 10^{-17} \, J \qquad (5.2)$$
deuterium tritium helium

Deuterium (hydrogen-2, $\,^{2}_{1}H$) comprises 0.015% of the hydrogen atoms in natural waters, so it is abundant in the oceans. The oceans contain 4.2×10^{13} tonnes of deuterium which, if extracted, could produce $3.4 \times 10^{30} \, J$ of energy when fused, a factor of 10^7 greater than the fossil fuel bank. Tritium (hydrogen-3, $\,^{3}_{1}H$) does not occur naturally, but is produced in nuclear fission reactors that use water as moderator or coolant (Section 2.1.2). It is also a by-product of the nuclear fusion process itself, when neutrons liberated by fusion are captured by lithium atoms forming part of the containment system of the reactor.

Thus although the process is *fusion* of light elements, not fission of heavy ones, if tritium is used there is some radioactivity in the fuel (tritium is radioactive with a half-life of 12 years), and bombardment of fusion reactor vessels by neutrons and other subatomic particles would give rise to a radioactive waste problem — though on a much smaller scale than that associated with fission reactors.

The main problems in sustaining fusion reactions are that (a) nuclei must be brought to within 10^{-15} m of each other before the strong nuclear attractive forces can overcome electrostatic repulsions, and (b) to achieve the necessary kinetic energies, temperatures of about 10^8 °C are required.

The maintenance of very high temperatures and the containment of the fuel at appropriately high pressures in fusion reactors are opposing requirements which have defeated many attempts to harness this energy source. Nevertheless, if the technological problems are solved — and best estimates say that this will be in the early decades of the twenty-first century at the earliest — then future energy scenarios could look very different from those we have been discussing. In the mid-1990s, however, cuts in the US fusion research budget suggested that the outlook was not promising.

If nuclear fusion or other alternative energy resources were to become widely developed in place of conventional hydrocarbon resources, this would lead to the question: what can be used to fuel smaller self-contained power units? The convenience of the petrol engine has resulted in its proliferation across the face of the Earth. Clearly, a transportable fuel is needed and, again, hydrogen could come to the fore as both a substitute for petrol and a means of storing energy until it is needed.

5.2.2 The hydrogen economy

Outside the sophistication of a fusion reactor, the use of hydrogen as a fuel depends quite simply on the reaction:

$$2H_2 + O_2 = 2H_2O \qquad (5.3)$$

which takes place when hydrogen is burnt in air and is exothermic, yielding $1.21 \times 10^8 \, \text{J kg}^{-1}$, roughly twice the calorific value of petroleum products ($0.5 \times 10^8 \, \text{J kg}^{-1}$ for petrol). Hydrogen is thus a non-polluting fuel with high 'energy density'. There are just two problems — the density of liquid hydrogen is ten times less than that of petrol, and hydrogen boils at $-253\,°C$ (20 K) — so there are major, but not insoluble, difficulties of transport and storage.

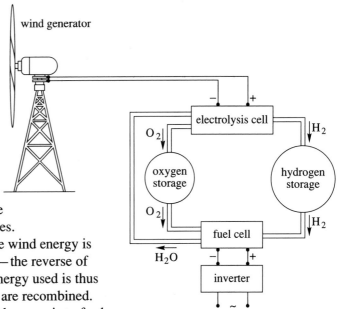

Hydrogen can also be used as a storage medium to smooth out the vagaries of unpredictable fluctuations in energy supply from renewable sources. Figure 58 illustrates the storage concept; in this case wind energy is used to electrolyse water into its component gases — the reverse of Equation 5.3 and so an endothermic process. The energy used is thus 'stored' in the gases and can be released when they are recombined. Burning the hydrogen is one way of doing this; another way is to feed hydrogen to the anode and oxygen to the cathode of a **fuel cell**, where they are recombined into water. As a result of ionization processes there is a transport of ions between the electrodes of the cell and a flow of electrons in the external circuit, producing a usable direct electric current. The inverter shown in Figure 58 is required to convert this to alternating current for use on an electricity supply grid.

Figure 58 Storage of unpredictably fluctuating energy supplies from wind generators (or from any other source) may be achieved by electrolysis of water into its component gases followed by their recombination in a fuel cell at times when electrical energy is required.

Electrolysis is just one of several methods by which hydrogen for fuel cells could be produced; other processes involve the thermochemical splitting of water by high-temperature chemical reactions and the biochemical liberation of hydrogen by certain kinds of plants and algae during photosynthesis. All three processes form part of a futuristic integrated system based on hydrogen as the energy carrier (Figure 59) and known as the **hydrogen economy**. Rather than being liquefied, gaseous hydrogen could be stored in high-pressure vessels or as metal hydrides; or in the longer term, perhaps, in depleted aquifers or oil wells. Whether nuclear fusion is harnessed or not, the hydrogen economy offers a promising alternative to the present fossil fuel economy. Nuclear fusion and the hydrogen economy are both a long way from conventional energy scenarios.

Figure 59 Elements of the hydrogen economy. Energy sources are shown at the top, conversion methods in the middle and the storage, distribution and use of hydrogen at the bottom.

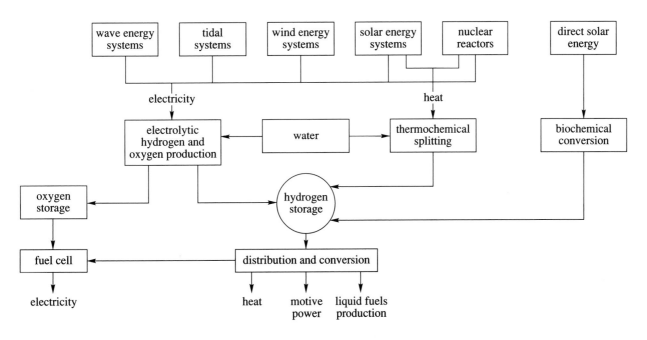

5.2.3 So where do we go from here?

Anyone who believes that exponential growth can go on forever in a finite world is either a madman or an economist.

Kenneth Boulting

A crisis is commonly a long-term problem not faced soon enough… So far, the American public demands more fuel than any other nation at prices lower than other nations pay.

Craig Hatfield

At the 1992 Earth Summit at Rio de Janeiro, representatives from some 170 nations (including several heads of state) undertook to compile a 'sustainable development plan' by the end of 1993, showing how energy and other resources (including water), transport, trade, biological diversity, agriculture and fisheries could all be managed to maintain the quality of life for future generations. Among other recommendations, the industrialized nations agreed to stabilize emission of carbon dioxide (from fossil fuels) at 1990 levels by the year 2000.

● Would that stop the increase in the concentration of atmospheric CO_2?

○ No. Stabilization at 1990 levels means merely that the atmospheric concentration of CO_2 would increase by the same amount each year — a net annual addition of some 10^{10} tonnes of CO_2.

The words *sustainability* and *sustainable development* have become particularly fashionable since then. The significance and implications of these concepts were lucidly summarized in Block 1 *Physical Resources*, along with examples of how, during the 1990s, growing numbers of people in the affluent societies of Western Europe, North America and Australasia had begun to 'think globally, act locally', initiating and supporting programmes of materials recycling, energy conservation and efficiency, waste reduction, and so on.

Let us look again at what sustainable development really means. In brief, as we read in Block 1 *Physical Resources*, it means development within our ecological means, as inhabitants of the Earth's biosphere managed to do for billions of years, until about 100 000 years ago, when modern humans began consciously and deliberately modifying their environment, setting the species on its way to modern civilization.

To put it more explicitly, sustainable development must eventually mean:

- phasing out extraction of non-renewable resources;
- stopping the depletion of renewable resources;
- recycling all manufactured materials;
- releasing all anthropogenic wastes at rates commensurate with natural cycles.

More use of recycled and biodegradable materials, more use of renewable energy sources, and greater energy efficiency, will all help to prolong the lifetime of fossil and nuclear fuels. But true sustainability will not even begin to be achievable until humanity sheds its strong addiction to non-renewable energy resources. In the mid-1990s there was little evidence that this addiction might be weakening. Thus:

1   More than three quarters of global energy consumption came from fossil fuels, over a third from oil (Figure 52). The low price of oil, however (Figure 53) meant the multinational companies were developing and improving recovery in existing fields rather than exploring actively for new ones. They were also seeking to expand their activities into countries of the former Soviet Union, which (as we know from Block 4 *Energy 1*) have large reserves of oil and particularly of natural gas. In the longer term there are other regions to be explored. For example, a potentially enormous and highly lucrative target is the Falklands Basin, where conditions are at least as hostile — and therefore as costly to deal with — as in the North Sea. Such an enterprise would not even be contemplated unless a market could be assured for 20–30 years at least.

2   There was continued growth in global air traffic, with new airports and extensions to existing ones under construction in several places. Aircraft manufacturers were planning to build a new generation of supersonic airliners and of long-range wide-bodied 600-seater jets. Emissions from aircraft engines already make a significant contribution to increased concentrations of CO_2 in the atmosphere, and there is new evidence that emissions of nitrogen oxides from high-flying aircraft might further deplete the stratospheric ozone layer.

3   The UK Government was planning for a doubling of motor vehicle production (mainly cars) by the year 2030, and had embarked on a major road-construction programme to accommodate the increased traffic. The programme met with considerable public resistance, but to keep the record straight we should perhaps recognize that the scale of protest was probably nothing like that which greeted original construction of the canal and rail networks in the late eighteenth and early/mid nineteenth centuries. All the same, it may have had some success, for the roads programme was scaled down. However, at the same time the Government was subdividing the national rail network in readiness for returning it to the private sector, a policy which many observers believed would lead to closure of rail links in more remote regions. The implication was that the respective upward and downward trends for road and rail transport in Figure 60 would continue. Meanwhile, motor manufacturers in Europe, North America and Japan continued their expansion, both at home and into developing markets, especially those of central and eastern Europe and Asia. The motor racing industry continued to thrive.

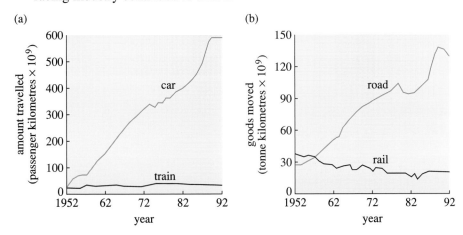

Figure 60   Trends in motor vehicle and rail use in Britain since the 1950s: (a) passengers, kilometres travelled; (b) freight goods, kilometres moved.

4   Total electrical generating capacity in Britain was set to increase, nearly all of it provided by fossil and nuclear fuels, though with some change in relative contributions (Figure 61) following the 'dash for gas' (Section 5). It was anticipated that by the end of the decade, the share of total energy contributed from renewable sources in Britain would have trebled to 3% (about 1.5 GW).

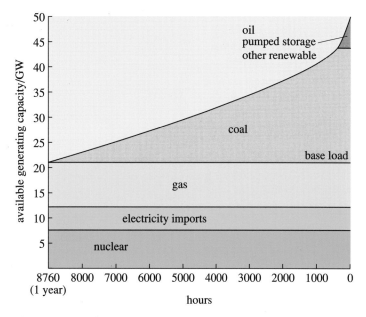

Figure 61   The proposed proportion of electricity generated from different sources in UK in the mid-1990s. Note increases from gas and imports relative to coal, compared with Figure 56.

5   The nuclear industry in Britain had increased its share of the electricity market and was discussing plans to start construction of up to three new power stations within the next decade. Meanwhile, the THORP plant (Section 2.3.2) was processing spent nuclear fuel and producing plutonium, of which there was a world surplus and which could only be used for atomic weapons and in fast breeder reactors — except for the small amounts mixed with uranium in MOX fuel. The International Atomic Energy Authority was campaigning for more electricity to be generated from nuclear energy.

To what extent do examples 1 to 5 above suggest compliance with undertakings made at the Rio Summit to stabilize CO_2 emissions at 1990 levels by the end of the millennium?

It is a question of balance. On the one hand, vehicles, aircraft, buildings, electrical appliances and so on are becoming more fuel-efficient as energy conservation technology develops, and as a greater share of electricity generation comes from more efficient fossil-fuel stations and/or from nuclear and alternative sources. On the other hand, there is evidence that numbers of both vehicles and aircraft continue to grow worldwide. As we noted earlier, however, even if stabilization is achieved, atmospheric CO_2 concentrations will continue to increase.

There are many other environmental side-effects of using fossil and nuclear fuels, and these are likely to go on increasing also, irrespective or whether or not CO_2 emissions are stabilized. They are most likely to increase (and at the greatest rates) in Asia, Africa, South America and eastern Europe, where few of the developing economies can afford the stringent environmental safeguards that those of us in the rich industrialized countries take almost for granted. For example, we saw in Section 2.3.1 that safety standards in the nuclear industries of eastern Europe are not as high as they might be. Acid rain, explosions in coal mines, rig blow-outs, and tanker spills are some of the well-publicized consequences of our addiction to fossil fuels.

A sustainable energy scenario?

For true sustainability as defined earlier in this Section, we must ultimately do without non-renewable and polluting fossil and nuclear fuels; this must inevitably mean large reductions in energy consumption and corresponding increases in energy efficiency.

 Why is that?

 The principal reason is the low 'energy density' of renewables compared with fossil and nuclear fuels. That means that large areas of land are required for significant quantities of energy to be produced.

Some elements of the hydrogen economy (Figure 59, though without the fusion component) would figure prominently in any sustainable energy scenario, supported by other forms of renewable energy, such as those outlined in Section 4 of this Block — bearing in mind that all materials used in any installations would themselves need to be completely recyclable.

In theory, we could start tomorrow and have the process completed in a few decades, perhaps less, for the *technology* to establish such a scenario is already available. No new inventions or 'technological breakthroughs' are required, although they could help enormously. For example, developments in information and communication technology are such that in the not too distant future people may have much less need to travel — and a large proportion of energy consumption goes in transport. Were superconductors to become a commercial reality, the energy needs for many types of vehicles and machinery could fall by an order of magnitude or more. Naturally, such developments also help the conservation of conventional energy resources, but the proportional contribution to a sustainable scenario would be much greater.

However, there can be little doubt that reliance on fossil and nuclear fuels will continue to be a feature of energy scenarios — be they of technological-fix or low-growth type — for a considerable time to come.

Throughout the world there are presently very few economic or political incentives to move away from the dominance of these non-renewable but convenient sources of energy, not least because (as any energy economist will tell you) the capital investment needed to change the basis of global energy supplies is so vast that it will take 30–50 years to accomplish such a change. Moreover, we know from Block 4 *Energy 1* and previous Sections of this Block, that supplies of fossil and nuclear fuels *at affordable prices* will be sufficient to sustain our energy requirements for many decades, probably centuries — especially if they are helped by more recycling, improved energy efficiency and conservation technologies, better waste management practices and so on.

Any real impetus for moving towards truly sustainable energy scenarios in the foreseeable future must depend upon how much we believe in and share the environmental concerns expressed at the Rio Summit. In short, how much do we really want '… to maintain the quality of life for future generations'?

Activity 4

1 To what extent do you think the energy policy set down in Activity 3 meets the basic criteria for sustainable development?

2 There has been some advocacy (particularly in the USA) of the electric car as a means of reducing emissions from fossil fuels and hence of moving towards sustainability. What criteria would you consider essential for any such developments to be considered truly sustainable?

3 Cars could also be fuelled by hydrogen or by liquid biofuels. The question is, could such fuels — which are of course renewable resources — sustain present-day traffic densities? In the mid-1990s, Britain consumed some 24 million tonnes or about 32×10^9 litres of motor fuel each year.

   (a) The yield of liquid biofuel from biomass crops is of the order of 1000 litres per year per hectare. What area of ground would be needed to produce the equivalent of mid-1990s consumption, assuming equivalence of energy conversion?

   (b) Liquid hydrogen is much less dense than conventional motor fuel, and we would need about 120×10^9 litres of it to match present consumption levels in the UK (assuming equivalence of energy conversion). Rough calculations based on the energy of the reaction:

   $$2H_2O \rightleftharpoons H_2 + O_2$$

   and data such as those in Table 5 suggest it might be possible to obtain of the order of 500 litres of liquid hydrogen fuel per year per m^2 of surface area, using solar energy in favourable locations. What sort of area would be needed to produce the required quantity of hydrogen fuel?

   (c) What is the biggest problem with hydrogen as a transportable fuel?

4 (a) For every bottle of Scotch whisky produced, the equivalent of four or five bottles of liquid waste rich in organic matter are produced. Environmental regulations prevent the liquid wastes from being dumped into rivers or the sea, and they are now pumped to a digester to produce biogas and generate electricity. Why does this laudable development represent only a small concession to the basic requirements of sustainability?

   (b) Could a truly sustainable scenario feature buildings 'coated' with photovoltaic cells to make them autonomous energy units?

5.3   Summary of Section 5

1 The UK Government's pit closure plan in late 1992 provided a classic example of how a high-value resource can be rendered worthless overnight by economic and political factors that are independent of geological availability. Such abrupt changes make forward planning difficult, especially in the energy industries.

2 Energy planning or forecasting must take into account not only the magnitude of possible future demand but also the availability of energy sources to provide it. In practice, most scenarios are either *historical,* making use of past trends and extrapolating them, or *technological fix,* having regard to development of more efficient ways of using and conserving energy. They are not mutually exclusive, and optimum forecasting is achieved by making use of both approaches.

3   Forecasting is especially necessary for electricity because of the long
    lead times for building power stations, and because the electricity supply
    industry must have a range of different types of plant to cope with
    fluctuations in demand, both daily and seasonal. It must also have excess
    capacity to deal with breakdowns or with unexpected high seasonal
    demand. The base load is normally supplied by nuclear power stations
    because they are not easily closed down for short periods.

4   No matter how carefully scenarios of future energy (or other resource)
    use are compiled, unforeseen political, economic and technological
    developments almost invariably render them inaccurate after a few years.
    For example, projected large increases in coal and nuclear energy in the
    UK by the year 2000, made in the late 1970s, could not have anticipated
    the effects either of the miners' strike of 1984–85 or of the Chernobyl
    disaster in 1986. An earlier forecast of exponential increase in
    replacement of coal by oil as the dominant fossil fuel, made in the early
    1970s, could not have anticipated the oil price rises of the mid-1970s.

5   Energy demand can be limited by improving efficiency of conversion of
    energy (more fuel-efficient engines, etc.) and by taking energy
    conservation measures (e.g. house insulation, vehicle speed limits, more
    public transport). CHP schemes can be up to 90% efficient, compared
    with 30% for conventional power stations.

6   Available energy sources all have drawbacks which limit their
    usefulness. Fossil fuels contribute to global warming and acid rain;
    nuclear fuels produce radioactive wastes; most 'alternatives'
    (renewables) require large areas of land and do not provide transportable
    fuels. Nuclear fusion and/or an energy economy based on hydrogen
    could provide almost limitless 'clean' energy.

7   Sustainable development in relation to energy resources must eventually
    mean doing without fossil and nuclear fuels, and relying entirely on
    renewable energy, including hydrogen. This would entail also massive
    reductions in energy consumption and great improvements in energy
    efficiency.

OBJECTIVES

Now that you have completed this Block, you should be able to do the following.

1   Explain in your own words, and use correctly, the terms in the *Glossary* relating to Block 4 *Energy 2*.

2   Perform simple calculations, use formulae and equations, plot and interpret graphs, and evaluate tables of data relating to different aspects of energy resources, i.e. reserves and resources, ore grades and tonnage, costs and prices, power outputs and efficiency, contributions to energy requirements, forecasting, etc.

3   Explain the distinction between energy obtained from combustion, from nuclear fission and from nuclear fusion, and summarize the difference between burner and fast breeder reactors.

4   Distinguish between primary and secondary uranium deposits, and outline why uranium is classified as an incompatible element that tends to be concentrated in granitic magmas, hydrothermal solutions and organic-rich sediments.

5   Summarize and explain (a) the fluctuating fortunes of the nuclear power industry and hence of uranium mining, (b) the effects of lead times on major projects (especially THORP), and (c) the relative importance of political, social and geological factors involved in underground disposal of radioactive wastes.

6   Distinguish hyperthermal, semi-thermal and hot dry rock resources in terms of geological setting and exploitation potential, and outline the main technologies used to optimize energy extraction efficiency and minimize environmental impacts.

7   Explain (a) why most surface energy resources ('alternatives') are relatively 'dilute', requiring large areas of land (or water) and quantities of constructional materials for large-scale power generation; (b) why these energy sources are not all environmentally benign; and (c) why they can never provide more than a fraction of global energy requirements.

8   Summarize the difficulties of forecasting energy demand and show how the politics and economics of resources are more important than geological and/or environmental factors in determining how the resources are used.

9   Explain why sustainable energy scenarios are still many decades away.

ANSWERS TO QUESTIONS

Question 1

In one year, 1 kg of uranium-238 simply undergoing spontaneous radioactive decay will produce 3×10^3 J, whereas 1 kg of coal is equivalent to 2.8×10^7 J. So it would take $(2.8 \times 10^7 \text{ J y}^{-1})/(3 \times 10^3 \text{ J}) \approx 9300$ years, or about 10^4 (10 000) years, for ordinary radioactive decay to produce the energy equivalent of the same mass of coal.

Question 2

All but 5000 tonnes of that huge quantity of mined rock will be waste. Because there is a difference of three orders of magnitude between tonnage of ore mined and tonnage of uranium yielded, the amount of waste is also 1.7 million tonnes. Specifically: $1\,700\,000 - 5000 = 1\,695\,000 = 1.7 \times 10^6$ to two significant figures.

Question 3

In both cases, low-density fluids (oil, gas, heated water) rise towards the surface, making use of primary or secondary permeability, according to the nature of the rocks. If the rising fluids encounter an impermeable layer, this acts as a barrier to upward migration. In the case of oil and gas, the fluids can accumulate beneath the barrier (the seal), and remain there more or less indefinitely. In the case of hydrothermal solutions, after the hot water has spread out, cooled, and deposited its minerals, it eventually leaves the system, percolating along minor cracks and fissures towards the surface.

Question 4

In the average underground mine it *costs* $120 per *tonne* to produce uranium which is *sold* at $40 per *kilogram*. Therefore $120/40 = 3.0$ kg of uranium must be produced from every tonne of ore mined. This is a grade of $3.0/1000 \times 100$ (%) or 0.3% uranium (3000 p.p.m.)

Question 5

(a) Perhaps the most important factor in the increased costs of production shown in Figure 20 was inflation following the oil price rise of 1974. However, part of the reason could also be lower ore grades, because more rock must be processed for a given yield of metal (in this case uranium), requiring increased expenditure on equipment, energy, water, and so on. So increasing costs, as signified by deepening colour in Figure 20, could at least partly be correlated with decrease in ore grade.

(b) No. It is more likely that production costs rose primarily because of inflation (see (a)), moving reserves from lower cost categories into higher cost categories. For example, the disappearance in 1977 of uranium priced at $20 kg^{-1} does not imply that *all* the resources in this category during 1968 to 1976 had been extracted, merely that what was left had became more costly to extract.

(c) Yes. Histograms portraying estimated extraction costs follow quite well both the rise and fall in the price curve. It is interesting to see that the uranium mining industry was so bullish in the late 1970s that resources costing more than $250 kg^{-1} to extract were identified — further dramatic price increases must have been expected.

(d)

(i) See Figure 62. There was a relatively stable supply–demand situation during the 1960s, with only a modest growth of nuclear power — this was at time when oil was hugely abundant and cheap. Following the oil price crisis, demand increased and the equilibrium price rose, enabling more resources to be classified as reserves (as well as encouraging exploration). The second half of the 1970s was a boom time for uranium and nuclear power. By the late 1980s, however, the market was depressed, with few (if any) new reactors being built, and huge surpluses of uranium supplies.

Note that we have drawn the demand curve for the 1980s *below* that for the 1960s, because in real terms the market price of uranium was probably lower then than in the 1960s.

(ii) Figure 19 shows that uranium ores generally occur in regions remote from their end-use locations. Uranium has low place value, because it commands a relatively high price and so is worth transporting long distances from its place of origin.

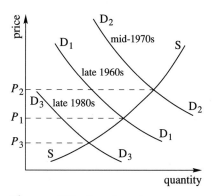

Figure 62 Supply–price curve (S) and three demand–price curves (D$_1$ to D$_3$) for the late 1960s, mid-1970s and late 1980s, with the three equilibrium prices (P_1 to P_3). Arbitrary scales.

Question 6

Clay-rich sedimentary rocks occur in the Mesozoic–Tertiary basins of Hampshire, London and the Yorkshire–Lincolnshire–Home Counties areas, and among the Palaeozoic rocks of central Wales, the Lake District, the southern uplands of Scotland, and Northern Ireland. The older rocks might provide the better disposal sites as they are more compact and stable and have undergone low-grade metamorphism to slates.

Appropriate salt deposits of Permo-Triassic age underlie the Midlands, particularly the Cheshire area, Dorset and the North Sea.

Hard Palaeozoic and Precambrian crystalline rocks are generally found in the upland regions of Wales, northern England and northern Scotland.

Question 7

(a)

(i) In Section 2.1.1 we explained that in a burner reactor the chain reaction depends entirely on fission of uranium-235 nuclei, which capture only slow neutrons. But fission of a uranium-235 nucleus produces both fast and slow neutrons. The fast neutrons must therefore be *slowed down* so that they can be captured by other uranium-235 nuclei.

(ii) Although a large number of neutrons is required to keep the chain reaction going (uranium-235 constitutes only one atom in 40 even in enriched uranium fuel), their action must be controlled. An unlimited number of neutrons would cause the fission of all the uranium-235 at once, which would be an atomic explosion. Excess neutrons above a certain number must therefore be *absorbed*.

(b) The breeder reactor (Equation 2.3) depends on the ability of fast neutrons to transmute uranium-238 into plutonium-239, and to sustain the fission of plutonium. Because the moderator in burner reactors is designed to *slow down* fast neutrons produced in the chain reaction, it is out of place in a breeder reactor.

(c) In burner reactors, most of the fast neutrons are moderated or absorbed — but it is not possible to remove them all. Those that remain can be captured by uranium-238, which forms the bulk of the fuel elements in all reactors, and plutonium is formed. The breeder reactor is expressly designed to produce plutonium, because it depends on the action of fast neutrons only, which turn uranium-238 into plutonium-239.

(d) Even in rich ore deposits, the uranium is 'diluted' by other elements in the minerals of the ore and surrounding rock. Nearly all neutrons are absorbed by other nuclides, i.e. the surrounding rocks act as a very effective set of control rods.

Question 8

A True. See discussion of incompatible elements, Section 2.2.1.

B True. See comments on vein-unconformity deposits, Section 2.2.1.

C False. Underground mining of veins generally will be more expensive in energy and staff costs than open-pit mining of sandstone-hosted uranium; see beginning of Section 2.2.2.

D True. See comments on roll-type uranium ores, Section 2.2.1.

E False. Yellowcake is impure uranium trioxide, Section 2.2.2.

F True. These are also the environments in which black shales form; see end of Section 2.2.1.

Question 9

(a) New fuel rods consist of pure uranium oxide which is radioactive but with a long half-life; spent fuel rods contain a few per cent of highly radioactive fission products, some of which have short half-lives, and so are intensely radioactive (see discussion of Figure 23).

(b) The aim of reprocessing is to re-enrich the uranium-235 in spent fuel rods for further use in burner reactors, to remove radioactive fission products, which act as unwanted moderators, and, more important, to extract plutonium for fast breeders. The uranium stockpiles that existed in the early 1990s because of uranium overproduction from mines, and the cancellation of the UK's fast breeder research programme both militated against the economic viability of reprocessing.

(c) Vitrification has two aims: first to concentrate HLW into a small volume for disposal, and second to lock the wastes into a relatively stable glass, which forms part of the multiple containment system resistant to groundwater penetration (Figure 24).

(d) Depleted uranium consists almost exclusively of uranium-238 which has a half-life of more than 4 billion years and therefore has a low level of natural radioactivity.

Question 10

(a) From the preceding text, rocks with low thermal conductivity are shales and many metamorphic rocks. If these are present within the top few kilometres, then the increase of temperature with depth will be more rapid than if high-conductivity strata were present (at constant q).

(b) You may have had to give this a little more thought, but from Section 2.2.1, which explains the geological distribution of one important radioactive element, uranium, you should realize that granite intrusions are the most likely source of above-average heat production in the crust — especially as granites typically contain more potassium and thorium than most other common rocks. Local heat flow anomalies might occur over such intrusions owing to the additional heat they add to the average, or background, heat flowing through the crust.

Of course, both (a) and (b) would provide better geothermal resources for exploitation if they occurred in regions where the background heat flow was also high, i.e. in semi-thermal rather than non-thermal areas.

Question 11

(a) In the first 12 years (1969–81) the capacity moved through approximately two doubling times (from 720 to 1440 and from 1440 to 2880 MW assuming an exponential rate). So the doubling time was 6 years. In the later 11 years (1981–1992) capacity almost exactly doubled again, to 5834 MW. The formula given for exponential growth is

$$\text{growth rate} \approx \frac{70}{\text{doubling time}}$$

Substituting 6 years gives a growth rate of 11.7% from 1969 to 1981 and substituting 11 years gives 6.4% from 1981 to 1992.

(b) Total geothermal power capacity in 1992 was $5834 + 4123 = 9957$ MW. That is close enough to $10\,000$ (10^4) MW to make a calculator unnecessary. The percentage contribution to world energy production is:

$$= \frac{10^4 \times 3.15 \times 10^{13} \times 100}{3.4 \times 10^{20}}$$

$$= \frac{3.15 \times 10^{19}}{3.4 \times 10^{20}}$$

$$= 0.09\%$$

Question 12

Assuming a surface temperature of 10 °C we would need to drill to $(150 - 10)/37 \approx 3.8$ km depth in south-west England.

Question 13

A   Answers 2 and 3; hyperthermal resources continue indefinitely so long as they are not overproduced, whereas geothermal heat is 'mined' from sedimentary basins and hot dry rocks.

B   Answers 1 and 3; steam is usually exploited for power generation in hyperthermal volcanic areas and this, too, is the objective of investigation of hot dry rocks (Section 3.3). Only hot water (about 60 °C, typically) is available in sedimentary basins.

C   Answer 3; this refers to the explosive stimulation and hydrofracturing techniques needed to create an artificial aquifer in hot dry rocks.

D   Answer 2; so far this is the only use for hot water pumped from sedimentary basins.

E   Answers 1 and 2; unless there is a seal, the natural geothermal aquifers in hyperthermal areas and sedimentary basins would 'leak'; this does not apply to hot dry rocks where the 'aquifer' is created artificially.

F   Answer 3; so far, rocks of this type have been the main focus of the exploration and development of hot dry rocks.

G   Answer 1; a steep geothermal gradient is most commonly provided by recent magmatic activity.

H   Answer 1; although the new technologies (2 and 3) have much to offer, they are most unlikely to overtake hyperthermal resource output (Table 4) for the foreseeable future.

I   Answers 1–3; all forms of geothermal energy result from heat generated inside the Earth.

Question 14

The possible disadvantage is that most biomass is of low density compared with coal and oil; much of it is carbohydrate rather than hydrocarbon, and it contains a high residual moisture content, even after drying (a process that itself uses energy). So its energy density (or calorific value) is very much lower than that of coal or oil. This means that comparatively large volumes of biomass will be required both as fuel and at the transportation and storage stages.

The environmental advantage is that the CO_2 produced by burning biomass is 'new' CO_2, which is recycled back into biomass by the growth of new vegetation, whereas fossil fuels release 'old' CO_2 trapped in vegetation tens to hundreds of millions of years ago, which increases the concentration of CO_2 in the atmosphere.

Question 15

(a) Incineration of domestic waste involves none of the four processes listed: the organic matter is burned directly as fuel.

(b) Landfill gas is biogas produced by digestion of organic matter under anaerobic conditions (item 3 in the list).

Question 16

Power output is given by $\frac{1}{2}\rho A v^3$ and we are told that $\rho = 1.3\,\text{kg m}^{-3}$, $A = 300\,\text{m}^2$ and $v = 10\,\text{m s}^{-1}$. So, power output at 80% efficiency is:

$$\tfrac{1}{2} \times 1.3 \times 300 \times 10^3 \times 0.8\ \text{J s}^{-1} = 0.156 \times 10^6\ \text{J s}^{-1} = 156\ \text{kW}$$

This is a 150 kilowatt generator (at this windspeed).

Question 17

(a) The industrialized nations have both the technological skills and the capital needed to undertake large hydroelectric schemes. The European countries have developed their hydroelectric potential most extensively with over 60% utilized and a further 20% planned or under construction. North America has also achieved 40% development, and South America has the most widespread developments in the non-industrialized world with nearly 20% of its potential operating or planned. In contrast, little use is made of hydropower resources in Africa or Asia.

(b) Countries with high mountain ranges and high annual rainfall are particularly favourable for hydropower development. Examples include western regions of North and South America, New Zealand and Alpine Europe. Such geologically young mountain ranges are not well endowed with fossil fuels, although there are coal basins in less mountainous parts of North America, Europe, the former USSR, China and Australia. The petroleum-rich countries of the Middle East and North Africa have little hydropower potential owing to their arid climates, and major oil and gas fields are almost by definition not particularly mountainous either.

Question 18

(a) The single direction generation scheme provides power for about 40% of the 25-hour cycle whereas double direction generation increases this potential to 50–55%. (Note that the combined periods for power output are not doubled because, in a single direction scheme, the water in the basin can be maintained at a higher average level than in a double direction scheme, and so power generation occurs for a longer period on the outgoing tide.)

Question 19

The mass of one mole of $C_6H_{12}O_6$ $(72 + 12 + 96\,g) = 180\,g$. On combustion, each mole will, theoretically, yield the $2.8 \times 10^6\,J$ that were required in its formation. So, $1\,kg$ $(10^3\,g)$ will yield:

$$\frac{10^3}{180} \times 2.8 \times 10^6\,J = 1.56 \times 10^7\,J$$

i.e. $15.6\,MJ\,kg^{-1}$, or about half the calorific value of bituminous coal.

Question 20

A False. Char is described as carbon-rich (Section 4.1.3) and has a calorific value of about $29\,MJ\,kg^{-1}$, roughly twice the value calculated for raw biomass in Question 19 and about the same as the value for coal.

B False. Equation 4.3 shows that the power developed by an aerogenerator depends on the density of air, the blade area and the wind speed, and not on the height or the location of the windmill. Although the air may be less dense on a hill, the wind is probably stronger.

C True. Energy can be stored by pumping water uphill to a storage reservoir during periods of slack demand and using the acquired gravitational potential energy to drive turbines during periods of peak demand.

D True. A tidal scheme may arise from a double or a single direction generator; often it is more economic to use the single direction type. On the other hand, half the energy from as oscillating water column converter would be lost (see Figure 49) if only a single direction generator was used.

Question 21

(a) Figure 29 (c) and (d) respectively. Double-flash (dual-flash) at Dixie Valley, binary cycle at Mammoth Lakes.

(b) About 3 km and 250 °C at Dixie Valley, about 200 m and 170 °C at Mammoth Lakes.

(c) The principal customer for Dixie Valley electricity is Bishop, California, 215 miles down the longest privately owned transmission line in the USA. That is probably the main reason for the high cost.

(d) The difference (60 MW as against 30 MW) is a consequence of the temperature difference (see item b) of the energy content of the geothermal fluid at the two sites.

(e) As the pressure falls, CO_2 escapes from solution, the pH rises, and calcium carbonate is deposited in the pipes, like scale in kettles.

(f) Binary cycle plants require the working fluid to be condensed and at Mammoth Lakes the condensers need to be air-cooled (with the help of fans). Cooling is less efficient on warm summer days. A 30-foot height restriction was imposed at the planning stage, and this further restricts air circulation and reduces efficiency.

Question 22

(a) Solar–thermal electricity from the Mojave plant costs about 12 cents per kWh compared with the average of about 4 cents per kWh from geothermal electricity in California.

(b) Output was reduced because stratospheric particles and sulphur dioxide aerosols from the Mount Pinatubo eruption reduced the intensity of solar radiation (worldwide, not just at this site). There were also more cloudy days than the average.

(c) A conventional gas-fired boiler is used to heat the water at night and on cloudy days.

(d) The big advantage is its flexibility and potential for small-scale use in remote locations. Maintenance is easy and there are no moving parts. Photovoltaic electricity is direct current, so an inverter is needed to convert to AC for conventional electrical power. The efficiency of photovoltaic conversion is still only of the order of 10%.

Question 23

(a) True. The process of formation of fossil fuels from plant material increases the proportion of carbon and hydrogen, and reduces the water content.

(b) Biomass burning releases CO_2 in the same way as fossil fuel combustion does, but the CO_2 is 'new' as opposed to 'fossil', and is recycled by new growth of biomass.

(c) Pyrolysis, controlled burning, anaerobic decay, or fermentation (Section 4.1.3) will all produce either liquid or gaseous fuels (or both) from biomass. The video shows generation of biogas by anaerobic decay of domestic and agricultural organic wastes.

Question 24

(a) Individual wind turbine towers require relatively small amounts of land area, and the space between them can be used for grazing or crop-growing.

(b) You would need 840/0.3 = 2800 such turbines to achieve the same rated output as the Wylfa power station.

Question 25

(a) Geothermal. The aquifers are not strictly renewable, as the rate of heat extraction exceeds the rate of reheating, so the aquifers cool down in a matter of decades; some gases are vented to the atmosphere.

Solar–thermal. Large areas of land are required (see Table 5); large amounts of metal and/or glass are required for the mirrors; the heat transfer fluid may leak from the system.

Photovoltaics. Quite large amounts of metals and glass and/or ceramics, as well as silicon, are required for the units, because of the (still) relatively low conversion efficiencies.

Biomass. Large areas of land are required to produce the biomass crops, and these would need to be monocultures, effectively 'sterilizing' land for other uses.

Wind: again large areas of land are needed (but see Question 24(a) above), as well as large amounts of metals and/or plastics and/or ceramics to make each unit — very large amounts for big wind farms such as that at Tehachapi Pass. In the early to mid-1990s in the UK there were protests about noise pollution and destruction of visual amenity by wind farms.

(b) The principal reason is the low energy density of virtually all renewable energies, compared with that of fossil fuels and particularly of uranium. Any move towards replacing fossil and nuclear fuels with renewables must be accompanied by drastic reductions in overall energy use, and greatly increased energy efficiencies.

Question 26

(a) Not surprisingly, actual total global energy production in 1990 was substantially less than predicted in 1971; about 3.5 (or 3.9, including 'non-commercials') $\times 10^{20}$ J, as against a predicted total of nearly 5.5×10^{20} J.

(b) The relative contributions of fossil fuels are rather different: about 40%, 22%, 26% for oil, gas, coal respectively, whereas the projected proportions were about 50%, 16% and 13%. The low projection for coal was a consequence of the very low oil price at the time, so that oil was perceived as replacing coal for many of its uses. The actual total fossil fuel consumption in 1990 (Figure 52) was about three-quarters of what was projected in 1971 (Figure 51).

(c) The nuclear share was projected to be more than double what it actually became in 1990 (about 0.4×10^{20} J against less than 0.2×10^{20} J); no prizes for guessing why, given the chequered history of the nuclear industry (e.g. Sections 2.1.4, 2.3.1), and concerns about the problems of nuclear waste (Section 2.3.3).

(d) The alternatives share (not including 'non-commercials') in 1990 was about double what was projected (0.2×10^{20} versus 0.1×10^{20} J), but it is still only a very small proportion of the overall total.

Question 27

(a) The DoE scenario saw a progressive rise in total energy consumption, almost doubling by 2025, with nuclear power the dominant energy source, backed up by coal. The marked decline in projected contributions from both oil and gas was presumably a recognition that coal reserves were far greater than those of oil and gas. Renewables were not considered likely to make a significant impact on the energy scene.

In contrast, the IIED scenario saw a progressive decline in total energy demand, with an energy scene dominated by coal and a reduced role for oil and gas by 2025 (as in the DoE scenario and presumably for the same reason), and for nuclear power as well. This scenario also predicted a marked rise in the contribution from renewables.

The DoE scenario forecast that electricity generation would more than double by 2025, whereas in the IIED scenario it remained more-or-less constant through the period.

(b) Perhaps the starkest contrast is the greatly diminished role of coal in 1990, which can be attributed partly to the political aftermath of the 1984 miners' strike and partly to environmental concerns about global warming and acid rain caused by emissions of CO_2 and sulphur oxides, coal being perceived as a 'dirtier' fuel in this regard than oil or gas. The contribution from oil grew less between 1976 and 1990 than might have been expected from the huge increase in motor vehicle traffic during the 1980s. The other big surprise is natural gas, consumption of which in 1990 was already far greater than anything envisaged in either scenario. North Sea gas was piped throughout virtually the whole country during the 1980s, becoming an important fuel for industry as well as for domestic heating and cooking. Many people preferred it to electricity for these purposes, which would account in part for the relatively modest increase in electricity in 1990.

Question 28

(a) If the loan period is increased, the interest rate could be reduced (it does not necessarily follow that it would), and the cost per kWh could fall.

(b) If initial capital costs were greater, then cost per kWh would also be greater.

Question 29

Perhaps most fascinating is the almost conservative pattern of relative changes in energy use envisaged by the two scenarios. In 1976 it was envisaged that by AD 2000;

- industry would increase its share slightly;

- domestic users would significantly reduce their share of energy consumption, perhaps a consequence of energy conservation in the home;

- commercial users (shops, offices, theatres, etc.) would likewise reduce their share, but not to such a marked degree, presumably for the same reasons;

- transport's share would only increase very slightly, and interestingly, would do so more in the IIED 'low-growth' scenario than in the DoE 'high growth' one.

The 1990 picture is startlingly different for industry and transport, relative to 1976.

- Industry's share fell by over a third, a consequence of the closure of a large proportion of heavy engineering, ship-building, steel-making, etc. during the early to mid-1980s.

- Transport's share increased by about a third, reflecting the huge increase in domestic car use, the transfer of much rail freight to roads, and the rise in air travel.

On the other hand, both the domestic and commercial share of energy consumption changed only slightly relative to 1976, but both trends are contrary to predictions for the year 2000. The overall 1990 picture shows a pattern very different from the predicted scenarios, and it is clear that the forecasters could have had no inkling of impending socio-political economic changes and how they would affect energy use.

Bear in mind, however, that Table 10 shows relative *proportions* of energy use, and contains no information about actual amounts of energy used. Those data are summarized in Table 7.

ANSWERS TO ACTIVITIES

Activity 1

1 Prices rose very sharply from $15 kg^{-1} to over $100 kg^{-1} in 1974–75 (peaking at over $110 kg^{-1} in 1979), while production took 5–6 years to reach its peak in 1980–81. The lag represents the *lead time* required to expand production at existing mines and to bring new mines on stream.

2 The Middle East 'oil crisis' of 1974 and subsequent years was the principal reason. It focused attention on the urgent need to develop non-hydrocarbon energy resources. Nuclear energy was an obvious answer; many new power stations were planned and developed, rapidly increasing the demand for uranium. Deposits that previously were uneconomic suddenly became viable, and widespread exploration led to the discovery of new deposits on a world scale. Uranium mining became a boom industry undergoing rapid expansion with the opening of new mines and a doubling of world production over a period of 5 years.

3 Uranium prices fell sharply in 1979–80 (from over $110 kg^{-1} to about $70 kg^{-1}), partly because environmental objections to nuclear power were beginning to take hold (Section 2.1.4); and you may recall that the Three Mile Island accident occurred in 1979. In addition, the anticipated rate of growth in energy demand, forecast in the late 1970s, just did not happen. Plans for new power stations were cancelled, uranium was over-produced and the industry went into decline.

The small 'blip' in prices (detectable also in the production histograms) in the early 1980s was probably a consequence of another 'mini oil crisis'. It was in a period of some turbulence so far as the UK was concerned — the Falklands War had just happened, and the coal miners were about to strike for a year; but while these events could have contributed to the fluctuations, they would not have been the primary cause of a global change in uranium prices.

4 Chernobyl blew up in 1986, but there is no sign of any effect in Figure 19. This could be construed as evidence that even so great a catastrophe (Section 2.3.1) had a negligible effect on an already much depressed industry.

Prices and production were still in decline well into the 1990s, as the same environmental tensions continued to cast a shadow over nuclear power generation in most countries.

5 In 1970 the price of uranium was around $15 kg^{-1}, while in 1989 it was approaching $40 kg^{-1}. Allowing for inflation in the intervening period, at a conservatively estimated average rate of 10% per year, prices would have doubled every seven years (70/10 = 7). Roughly speaking that would make the price $30 kg^{-1} in 1977, $60 kg^{-1} in 1984, and well over $100 kg^{-1} by 1989. So a price of less than $40 kg^{-1} represents a considerable fall in real terms.

(You may disagree with the average inflation figure, but the principles remain the same.)

6 US production was well over half the world total in 1970 (about 10 000 tonnes out of a total of about 17 000 t), against about an eighth by 1989 (about 4000 t out of a total of about 33 000 t). As indicated in the answer to item 3, the decline in the fortunes of the nuclear industry was more severe in the US than elsewhere.

7   The answer lies in the grade of the ore. If an underground mine is working higher grade ore, its costs per kg of uranium could still be more competitive than those of an open-pit operation extracting low-grade ore. Interestingly, the new high-grade ores, particularly those in vein-unconformity deposits, were able to dominate the market, leading to selective decline in mining of lesser grade ore. This had a greater effect on uranium production in the USA than elsewhere, though it is fair to add that some mines both there and elsewhere survived, either because they were regarded as of strategic national importance, or because they had contracted for long-term fixed price sales during the boom period.

8   1000 MW = 1 GW; to generate this amount requires some 160 tonnes uranium per year. So 320 GW require $320 \times 160 = 51\,200$ tonnes per year. This is significantly greater than the 33 000 tonnes or so produced in 1990. The shortfall (about 18 000 t) could easily be made up from the stockpile and indeed at a depletion rate of about 20 000 tonnes annually, the stockpile could last for about 7 years without any increase in mined new production. In fact, the existence of this vast stockpile, containing nearly three years forward reactor requirements, is a further reason why the uranium market was in a particularly depressed state in the early 1990s.

9   The concentration of uranium in a rock is the result of geological processes. It is not affected by price or market forces. These can only determine whether or not a particular concentration is high enough (and the tonnage large enough) to make extraction profitable. If the price rises, a uranium-bearing rock may become an ore; if the price falls again, that ore may revert to being just a uranium-bearing rock. The rocks themselves don't change; what changes is our perception of them as commodities.

Activity 2

This is not a 'right' explanation; it is merely an outline of points that could have occurred to you.

In most places, wind power cannot contribute as much as tidal power to regional/national needs, on account of the low 'energy density' of moving air: e.g. the power output from the Mersey barrage could only be obtained by many hundreds of wind turbines (see Section 4.2).

Wind turbines can be installed in a matter of a year or two, so they can be generating before significant levels of interest are incurred during construction, but they would probably require replacement after about 30 years. On the other hand, a tidal barrage would take 10 years to construct and would incur massive interest charges before even a penny was earned in generation. The risks are much greater, especially as the initial costs are higher than for wind power; and at the end of the long lead time it may not be possible to sell the electricity at the required 'pay-back' price. However, a tidal barrage would last for many decades, if not indefinitely, so in theory at least the electricity should become progressively cheaper with time.

Construction of a small to medium sized wind farm requires far less in the way of constructional and other raw materials than would a tidal barrier. But that is a reflection of the disparity in total output: to build enough wind turbines to produce the power generated by a tidal barrage would probably require comparable amounts of building materials.

Location of wind farms is more flexible than for tidal barrages, and there are fewer constraints on the scale of operation. Construction of a tidal barrage means commitment to a permanent site.

Apart from visual impact and some noise, wind farms have relatively little environmental impact, if flocks of migrating birds can be persuaded to steer clear of them. A tidal barrage changes an estuary forever, not necessarily for the better; and estuaries are very sensitive environments, rich in diverse wildlife.

Summary: The main reasons for the contrast would seem to be: greater flexibility of wind farms; more rapid return on investment and less danger of 'white elephantism'; and less chance of permanent environmental damage.

Activity 3

There are no 'right answers' to this Activity either, except perhaps for some of the minor details. Feel free to disagree with what follows.

1

(a) The policy does not mention oil because it is mainly about how electricity is to be generated — the author is in the electricity supply industry and may not regard oil as suitable for power generation, perhaps because he thinks it is more useful as chemical feedstock and vehicle fuel.

(b) 'Long-term' probably means a few decades (the date of 2040 is specifically mentioned at one point).

(c) There is probably enough gas in North Sea fields to meet demand over the next few decades, and the renewables potential is more than sufficient, provided that sites can be found for (say) more wind farms. There is plenty of nuclear fuel available, though of course it would have to be imported. Given the rate of run-down of the British coal industry in the 1990s (see Section 5.1), about half the coal required by this policy would have to be imported.

(d) The anticipated three-fold increase in electricity demand by AD 2040 must surely be for the world as a whole, not just the UK, where consumption went up by about 35% between 1976 and 1990 (Table 7). Even assuming linear growth at that rate, which is unlikely because of improved energy conservation and efficiency, consumption in the UK would be about 1.5×10^{18} J y^{-1} by 2040, which is not a three-fold increase. In fact, the tone of the article suggests that UK electricity demand would increase relatively slowly.

(e) The proposal focuses on electricity partly because the author is in the electricity supply industry, but perhaps mainly because the long lead times required to build power stations requires more forward planning than do most other parts of the energy supply industry.

The following points could have occurred to you when assessing the policy.

- In the assumption of increased demand for electricity no mention is made of improved energy efficiency or conservation measures (see below).

- Between 70 and 80% of electricity would still be generated by fossil fuels, with all that that implies about CO_2 emissions and global warming.

- '... up to four new PWR stations ... ordered over the next five years' could be difficult to achieve, given public concerns about the nuclear industry and problems of radioactive waste disposal.

- Trebling global electricity generation within a few decades could place massive reliance on nuclear and/or renewable energy, if the threat of global warming is to be avoided. There are problems with proliferation of nuclear power plants, see above, and large-scale use of alternatives would require huge areas of land; which might also be needed to accommodate the increased populations and to grow their food.

2   The object of this part of the Activity is to emphasize once more how political and economic factors can affect extraction and utilization of resources irrespective of their traditionally perceived intrinsic value or usefulness.

Reducing revenue tax and removing concessions on exploration expenditure would encourage (force?) oil companies to extract more oil from existing fields (by improving secondary and tertiary recovery techniques) and to cut back on their search for new fields. If this policy were maintained for a significant period, say 10 years, the price of oil would have to rise steeply, as existing fields become exhausted and extra funds were needed to explore for new fields. It is one way of extending the lifetime of oil reserves. Meantime, however, many exploration companies might go out of business, leaving fewer people available to look for new fields when the time came.

On the face of it, this would have little effect on the policy in the article, except that: (a) it could be extended to gas fields in the North Sea and (b) a significant rise in the price of oil (and gas) could affect prices of other components in the 'energy basket'.

3   Energy conservation is very important, especially if you include energy-saving appliances as well as improved standards of insulation, more use of public versus private transport, and so on (see Section 5.1.1). Unless energy savings become significant, however (say, more than about 10%), the overall 'mix' of energy sources is not likely to be very different from that discussed above.

The policies considered in part 2 of this Activity suggest that there can be economic distortions in other parts of the energy industry, which can hardly fail to affect what happens in the electrical sector.

In short, the policy outlined in the article should perhaps be seen as a contribution to part of a national energy policy that takes account of production and consumption of energy for all uses.

Activity 4

1   James Hann's policy set out in Activity 3 makes virtually no concessions to any sort of sustainability. Ninety-five per cent of UK energy would continue to be provided by non-renewable fossil and nuclear fuels, with only 5% from renewables. It is a plan for economic growth, and in all such plans environmental improvements inevitably have lower priority.

2   Here are some suggestions for 'sustainable' electric vehicles, not in any particular order.

- Sustainable energy scenarios mean doing with less energy (because of the low energy density of renewables), and using it very efficiently, so cars would have to be light and relatively slow and have high power-to-weight ratios.

- Batteries would need to be recharged, so centralized electricity generation would still be necessary, even if 'power stations' were smaller. This would also tend to limit the number of cars in use. 'Solar' cars would be independent of such a requirement, of course.

- Batteries and cars would have to be completely recyclable.

- A 'steady state' road system would be necessary, with materials being recycled into new carriageways as they deteriorated. An expanding road network would be out of the question. This would also limit car numbers.

3   The calculations suggest that very large areas of land would be needed, such that energy consumption would need to be much less profligate than it is today.

(a) If 10^3 litres can be produced from 1 hectare, then 32×10^9 litres would need $32 \times 10^9 / 10^3$ hectares $= 32 \times 10^6$ hectares.

There are 10^2 hectares per square kilometre, so the area of land required would be 32×10^4 km², an area greater than the whole of the UK.

(b) In this case, we can obtain 500 litres from 1 m², annually.

32×10^9 litres would need $32 \times 10^9 / 500 \, \text{m}^2 = 64 \times 10^6 \, \text{m}^2$

That is 64 km², an area 8×8 km square. Only in low latitude regions (like the Middle East?) would solar radiation be strong enough and sustained enough to produce those yields of hydrogen fuel.

(c) The biggest problem with hydrogen as a fuel is that it boils at $-253\,°C$, and would not be easy to store or transport in that form (see Section 5.2.2).

4

(a) Here are some reasons why this is only a small step towards sustainability. The whisky industry uses disposable glass and plastic bottles to market its products. Though both are recyclable, most still end up in waste tips. The industry must rely on fossil fuels to transport its products to markets all over the world, mainly by road within national boundaries (see Figure 60) and by air across boundaries. Advertising and marketing must use large amounts of energy, also paper (which can admittedly also be recycled, but see above). As the industry is based in Scotland, however, it is likely that power to run the distilleries themselves comes in large measure from hydroelectricity, as well as from any biogas they produce from their own wastes.

(b) Coating buildings with photovoltaic cells (or making windows out of 'photovoltaic glass'; see Video Band 13: *Renewable Energies*) is an excellent way of moving towards sustainability, provided that: all components are recyclable; the buildings are properly ventilated and insulated, so that while heating may be needed in winter, air conditioning should not be necessary in summer; provision is made for any surplus energy to be supplied to other users; and other energy-saving measures are adopted, including energy-efficient lighting and appliances.

Acknowledgements

The authors would like to thank the following for their helpful comments and suggestions on the earlier drafts: David Assinder, Godfrey Boyle, Sheila Dellow, David Elliott, Peter Scott. The following student readers are thanked for their comments on an early draft: Julia Adamson, Tom Denne and Iris Rowbotham.

Grateful acknowledgement is made to the following sources for permission to reproduce material in this block.

Figures

Cover: Satellite composite view of Earth, copyright © 1990 Tom Van Sant/ The GeoSphere® Project, Santa Monica, California, with assistance from NOAA, NASA, EYES ON EARTH, technical direction Lloyd Van Warren, source data derived from NOAA/TIROS-N Series Satellites. All rights reserved; *Figures 2, 4 and 6:* The Central Office of Information, *Pamphlet 28: Nuclear Energy in Britain*, © Crown Copyright. Reproduced with the permission of the Controller of Her Majesty's Stationery Office; *Figures 5 and 10:* Courtesy of Nuclear Electric; *Figure 9:* Blowers, A., Lowry, D. and Solomon, D. (eds) (1991) *The International Politics of Nuclear Waste*, Macmillan Press Ltd; *Figure 16(a):* International Uranium Resources Evaluations Project Report on Phase 1 (1980) *World Uranium Geology and Resource Potential*, Miller Freeman Publications; *Figure 21:* Gittus, J. H. *et al.* (1987) *The Chernobyl Accident and its Consequences*, United Kingdom Atomic Energy Authority; *Figure 23:* Johnson, K. D. B. (1980) in *Energy in the Balance: papers from the British Association meeting 1975*, Westbury House; *Figure 27:* Grindley, G. W. (1965) *The Geology, Structure and Exploitation of the Wairakei Geothermal Field, Taupo, New Zealand*, reproduced by permission of the Institute of Geological and Nuclear Sciences Limited; *Figure 30: European Directory of Renewable Energy*, James & James (Science Publishers) Ltd; *Figure 33: Publicity Chart of Heating System in Southampton*, Southampton Geothermal Heating Company Limited; *Figure 34:* Willes-Richards, J. *et al.* (1990) 'HDR Resource/Economics', in Baria, R. (ed.), *Hot Dry Rock Geothermal Energy*, © CSM Associates Limited; *Figure 36:* Long, G. *et al.* (1976) *Solar Energy – its potential contribution within UK: Department of Energy Paper No.16*, © Crown Copyright. Reproduced with the permission of the Controller of Her Majesty's Stationery Office; *Figure 38: The Independent*, 3rd April 1992; *Figures 39, 46 and 59:* Crabbe, D. and McBride, R. (1978) *The World Energy Book*, Copyright © Kogan Page and Contributors 1978, Kogan Page Limited, London; *Figure 45:* Department of Energy (1984) *Tidal Power from the Severn Estuary Volume 1*, © Crown Copyright. Reproduced with the permission of the Controller of Her Majesty's Stationery Office; *Figure 48:* Barnaby, F. and Barnaby, W. (1990) *Oceans of Wealth*, © Living Tapes Limited 1990, Videotel Marine International Ltd; *Figure 49(a):* Salter, S. H. (1976) 'Research and development news', in *NERC News*, **2**(3), December 1976, © Professor Stephen H. Salter; *Figure 49(b):* Kenward, M. (1976) in *New Scientist*, **70**, May 1976, IPC Magazines Ltd; *Figures 49(c) and 49(d):* ETSU/Department of Energy; Figure 50: 'Mining', *The Guardian*, 14th August 1993; *Figure 51:* Knowles, L. (1971) 'Earth's dwindling stock of fossil fuels', in *New Scientist*, **51**(563), 5th August 1971, IPC Magazines Ltd; *Figure 52:* Woodcock, N. H. (1994) *Geology and Environment in Britain and Ireland*, UCL Press Limited, © Nigel H. Woodcock 1994; *Figures 54 and 55:* 'Nuclear Power – the CEGB's planning records', in *The Ecologist*, **11**(6), 1981, Ecosystems Ltd; *Figure 56:* Parker, M. and Surrey, J. (1993) 'The genesis of the UK coal crisis', reprinted with permission from *Nature*, **361**(6414), 25th February 1993, Copyright 1993 Macmillan Magazines Ltd; *Figure 58:* Summers, C. M. (1971) 'The conversion of energy', in *Scientific American*, **224**(3), September 1971, reprinted with permission. Copyright © 1971 by Scientific American, Inc. All rights reserved.; *Figure 60:* Brown, P. (1994) ' 'Greenhouse' document targets cars and domestic fuel', *The Guardian*, 26th January 1994.

Physical Resources and Environment